# Proclamation 3

Aids for Interpreting
the Lessons of the Church Year

# Lent

## Pheme Perkins

Elizabeth Achtemeier, series editor

## Series B

FORTRESS PRESS   Philadelphia

Third printing 1987

**Library of Congress Cataloging in Publication Data**

Perkins, Pheme.
  Lent, series B.

  (Proclamation 3)
    1. Bible—Homiletical use.   2. Bible—Liturgical
lessons, English.   3. Lent.   I. Title.
II. Series.
BS534.5.P47 1984      220.6      84–6010
ISBN 0–8006–4103–5

3376J87    Printed in the United States of America    1–4103

# Contents

# Series Foreword

*Proclamation 3* is an entirely new aid for preaching from the three-year ecumenical lectionary. In outward appearance this new series is similar to *Proclamation: Aids for Interpreting the Lessons of the Church Year* and *Proclamation 2*. But *Proclamation 3* has a new content as well as a new purpose.

First, there is only one author for each of the twenty-eight volumes of *Proclamation 3*. This means that each author handles both the exegesis and the exposition of the stated texts, thus eliminating the possibility of disparity between scholarly apprehension and homiletical application of the appointed lessons. While every effort was made in *Proclamation: Aids* and in *Proclamation 2* to avoid such disparity, it tended to creep in occasionally. *Proclamation 3* corrects that tendency.

Second, *Proclamation 3* is directed primarily at homiletical interpretation of the stated lessons. We have again assembled the finest biblical scholars and preachers available to write for the series; now, however, they bring their skills to us not primarily as exegetes, but as interpreters of the Word of God. Exegetical material is still presented—sometimes at length—but, most important, here it is also applied; the texts are interpreted and expounded homiletically for the church and society of our day. In this new series scholars become preachers. They no longer stand back from the biblical text and just discuss it objectively. They engage it—as the Word of God for the worshiping community. The reader therefore will not find here the divisions between "exegesis" and "homiletical interpretation" that were marked off in the two earlier series. In *Proclamation 3* the work of the pulpit is the context and goal of all that is written.

There is still some slight diversity between the several lections and calendars of the various denominations. In an effort to overcome such diversity, the North American Committee on a Common Lectionary issued an experimental "consensus lectionary" *(The Common Lectionary)*, which is now being tried out in some congregations and which will be further altered at the end of a three-year period. When the final form of that lectionary appears, *Proclamation* will take account of it. In the meantime, *Proclamation 3* deals with those texts that are used by *most* denominations on any given Sunday. It also continues to use the Lutheran numbering of the Sundays "after Pentecost." But Episcopalians and Roman Catholics will find most of their stated propers dealt with under this numbering.

Each author writes on three lessons for each Sunday, but no one method of combining the appointed lessons has been imposed upon the writers. The texts are sometimes treated separately, sometimes together—according to the author's own understanding of the texts' relationships and messages. The authors interpret the appointed texts as these texts have spoken to them.

Dr. Pheme Perkins is Professor of Theology at Boston College. She received her Ph.D. from Harvard University and is the author of ten books and numerous articles, including *Ministering in the Pauline Churches* and (with Reginald Fuller) *Who Is This Christ?* She has served the editorial boards of the *Journal of Biblical Literature, Catholic Biblical Quarterly, Horizons,* and *Harper's Bible Dictionary,* and lectures throughout the United States and Canada.

# Ash Wednesday

| Lutheran | Roman Catholic | Episcopal | Pres/UCC/Chr | Meth/COCU |
|---|---|---|---|---|
| Joel 2:12–19 | Joel 2:12–18 | Joel 2:1–2, 12–17 or Isa. 58:1–12 | Isa. 58:3–12 | Isa. 58:1–12 |
| 2 Cor. 5:20b– 6:2 | 2 Cor. 5:20– 6:2 | 2 Cor. 5:20b– 6:10 | James 1:12–18 | James 1:12–18 |
| Matt. 6:1–6, 16–21 | Matt. 6:1–6, 16–18 | Matt. 6:1–6, 16–21 | Mark 2:15–20 | Mark 2:15–20 |

## FIRST LESSON: JOEL 2:12–19

The passage opens with a call to the people to return to the Lord in national repentance and prayer. The call answers the alarm sounded in Joel 2:1–11. Verses 18–19 express the hope that the Lord may turn aside the coming destruction, a food shortage (v. 19a) or the general distress of the "day of the Lord" (cf. v. 11). Joel has taken up the theme of returning to the Lord with all one's heart from Deuteronomy (4:28–31) and from earlier prophets (Amos 4:6–11; Hos. 3:5; 14:2; Jer. 3:10; 24:7). The Deuteronomic tradition of return to the Lord with all one's heart is contrasted with a false piety which might show itself in simply rending one's garment as in the mourning ritual. The earlier prophets called the people to turn away from a particular offense. The Deuteronomic tradition had presented return as special listening to the voice of the Lord in the Torah (Deut. 30:2, 8, 20).

Joel uses that understanding to recall the prophetic word of earlier times. He directs his message against the cultic community of Jerusalem, which prided itself in its fulfillment of the Torah. Joel reminds them that even though the community is flourishing as part of the Persian empire, they need to hear the call to return to the Lord. Without a period of renewal and repentance, the nation would lose its sense of the prophetic Word of God. Because they were part of a larger empire, the people did not face the external threats about which earlier prophets had spoken. The mood of the country was one of confidence. The people were sure of God's election and of the security of Jerusalem. Joel could not point to any particular national disaster to warn the people that they should repent. Instead, he finds that the character of God requires a period of turning back to the Lord.

Many scholars think that the calamity in chapter 2 is to be identified with the plague of locusts in Joel 1:12, 18. However, Joel 2:2 suggests that a new distress, never seen before, is to come upon Israel. In 2:11 the Lord approaches as the commander of the enemy hosts that are to overwhelm the nation. The call to repentance in chapter 2, then, is spoken in view of the new disaster of the day of the Lord. The promise of answer in v. 19 picks up both disasters. The return of grain in v. 19a reflects the plague in chapter 1, while verses 19b–20 promise to drive the foreign invaders from the land.

God's character provides motivation for repentance (vv. 12–14). God is gracious and merciful, slow to anger, abounding in *hesed* (steadfast love), and repents of evil (v. 13b). This list describes God's faithfulness to the covenant. Formulae such as Exod. 34:6–7 reflect similar attributes. The closest parallel to this phrase is Jon. 4:2. The announcement of catastrophe seeks to awaken in the hearers a sense of repentance so that God will not carry out the threat. "He repents of evil" shows the Lord as one who turns away from impending evil in response to such a conversion (also see Jer. 18:7–8; 26:3, 13, 19; 42:10; Exod. 32:12, 14; 2 Sam. 24:16). God never brings evil without cause. The evil is that which would otherwise be a consequence of violation of the covenant by the people. "Gracious" implies complete favor; the goodwill in which a superior condescends to an inferior (Exod. 22:26). "Merciful" evokes the care and anxiety of the parent for the helpless offspring. "Patient" implies restraint of anger. The most significant covenant term is *hesed,* variously translated as mercy, faithfulness, steadfast love. *Hesed* can refer to the great kindness of the Lord in creating the community through the covenant; to God's restraint of anger with the people for violating the covenant and to God's constant even "excessive" fidelity to that covenant.

The people cannot presume that their repentance will compel a response from God, since they deserve the evil which is to come. The "perhaps he will turn" is fundamental to the prophetic tradition of repentance. An acknowledgment of divine freedom is part of all prayer of petition. We cannot assume that our fasting or penance ever compels a divine response. Such presumption would destroy those attributes of divine love and mercy which are central to God's character.

The "perhaps" also warns the community that it stands under divine judgment. If the Lord does repent, the people will find itself "blessed." This blessing is described as the cereal and drink offerings appropriate to a covenant sacrifice. Since Joel is not speaking in a time of national political emergency, we are to see this national repentance as an acknowledgment of fundamental truths about God embodied in the covenant traditions and the prophetic heritage. The nation always stands in need of repentance under the uncertainty of divine judgment. At the same time, one can trust in the characteristics of mercy, *hesed,* "repenting of evil" that God has shown throughout Israel's history.

Verses 15–17 give instructions for turning to the Lord. No one is excluded from the summons. Blowing the horn signals the people to seek refuge in the Lord through fasting and assembly for prayer. The command to sanctify the people (v. 16a) implies that all are to be prepared for worship by ceasing work, by abstaining from sex, and by fasting. Even those who are normally exempt from other forms of public summons, such as that to Holy War—infants, small children, and newlyweds—must respond to this call. This time of repentance is even more important than a national disaster like a war.

Verse 17 describes the ritual of the assembly. The priests are to stand between the entrance to the great hall of the Temple and the altar of burnt offering. They are to make petitionary prayers to the Lord on behalf of the people. The Lord is reminded that the people are his property (RSV: "inheritance"). If God were to permit their destruction, it would be a reproach against their owner among all the nations of the world. This "shame" would be evident if the ruins of the destroyed Temple were left for all to see. The ruins would stand at the highest point in the city, where the great assembly was taking place.

The second section envisages the mockery that would follow God's abandoning the people. Other nations would say, "Where is their

God?'' This taunt shows that the catastrophe is more than economic or political disaster. It represents the end of the covenant relationship between God and the people. Thus, the prophet reminds those who feel secure in their possession of the Temple and its cult that they always live in radical dependence upon God. They only exist as a nation because of God's gracious election. Recall the question in v. 11b, "Who can survive the day of the Lord?" The earlier prophetic tradition already provided a clear answer: no one (Amos 5:18–20; Isa. 2:9–11).

Joel calls the community to nothing less than total reorientation. The question is whether God's coming will be in judgment or blessing. The prophet's message reminds the community that it can never allow the apparent prosperity and stability of the present to obscure its dependence upon God.

Verses 18–19 mark a turning point in the book. The oracles about the future now point to the continuation of God's love and mercy. Verse 18 links the earlier part of the book to what follows. The Lord is jealous for the people. In Zeph. 1:18 God's zeal or jealousy meant the coming of the evils of the day of judgment (1:18). Joel has transformed that tradition in a striking way. God's zeal is not against a sinful people but is jealousy on their behalf. It is manifest in another divine attribute, pity. Verse 19 begins a series of oracles that answer the plea made by the priests. The oracle of assurance continues through 3:5. God's first response is a sign of mercy in the fruits of the earth, the grain, wine, and oil that provide satisfaction for the people. Verse 19a reverses the conditions of famine. The next sign of divine mercy (vv. 19b–20) reverses the reproach which the world would have addressed to God if the people had been reduced to ruin. God will drive away the enemy nations so that the people are not destroyed.

Thus, while the call of alarm and the summons to national repentance have reminded the people of the possibility of divine judgment even in their time of great prosperity, the dominant vision is one of divine mercy and promise. This great liturgical drama in which the entire community turns to God in fasting and prayer provides the setting in which God's mercy, *hesed,* and graciousness toward the people is affirmed. This passage also reminds us that repentance is not response to an obvious evil or time of national crisis, but is grounded in a knowledge of the nature of God and of God's fruitful love for a people who can never claim to have deserved such mercy. It asks that we acknowledge our radical dependence upon God. This attitude goes far beyond lamenting our personal or collective sins. It suggests that we use Lent as a time to reflect upon the biblical experience of living in relationship to the gracious God of the covenant.

### SECOND LESSON: 2 CORINTHIANS 5:20b—6:2

This passage is part of a plea to the Corinthian community for reconciliation. Traveling missionaries had been preaching in Corinth and had led some people to reject Paul, the founder of the community. Paul's opponents seem to have presented Christianity as a religion that enabled its missionaries to give demonstrations of divine power through miracles and inspired speech. They carried with them letters from other communities attesting to the miracles that they had worked in those communities. It is easy to see the appeal of such a message. Much of the religious practice of the time emphasized the benefits to be derived from the gods. They were worshiped in impressive rituals and sacrifices. Throughout this section of 2 Corinthians, Paul has appealed to the crucified Christ as the true image of salvation. In 5:11-12, Paul says that he is not going to use human recommendations, but he does want to give the Corinthians reason to be proud of his ministry, "so that you may be able to answer those who pride themselves on a person's position and not on his heart." He insists that the Christian has new standards for evaluating what is worthwhile. Paul centers his vision on the cross as God reconciling a sinful world. Verse 20a points to the mission of Christ in the apostle as God's own appeal to humanity. Thus, when the Corinthians respond to Paul's plea for reconciliation, they are responding to God's plea. Reconciliation is more than a "one time" declaration that God does not count a person's sins. The reconciliation with God which comes to those who are "in Christ" must be expanded to embrace the life which they live after their baptism. It is an ongoing task of the Christian community. For Paul, the true apostle is not a person of impressive gifts of speech or healing. The true apostle is one who endures affliction but is never crushed by it. Paul concludes with a final appeal to the Corinthians. They are to turn from their fascination with the false apostles and demonstrate their affection for him. As the founder of the Corinthian community he is the source of their faith (6:11–12).

This passage addresses the message of reconciliation to a situation in which the Christian community was in need of reconciliation. When we consider the significance of repentance for our lives, we should consider the failure of reconciliation within our own communities. Reconciliation is not merely a matter of private flaws, imperfections, or quarrels. It can poison the life of an entire community as it did in Corinth, where the community was split by public divisions over the ministry of the apostle. Paul does not limit reconciliation to its social manifestations. Since it represents the reality of divine salvation, reconciliation is not a human creation. Rather, it expresses God's own activity as Creator. The appeal to "be reconciled" summons humans to engage themselves in that process and become ambassadors of reconciliation to the world. Paul uses a traditional formula in 5:21, which breaks into its context. The phrase "working together with him" in 6:1 picks up "on behalf of Christ" in 5:20. Paul warns that as long as the Corinthians persist in their alienation from the apostle and his message of the crucified Christ, then their "being in Christ" is worthless. This appeal is supported by a citation of Isa. 49:8 as though God is speaking directly. Like the prophets of old, Paul is presenting God's own claim for fidelity and obedience.

The formula presents a striking affirmation of Christ's role in God's reconciling creation: Christ the one who did not know sin, God makes sin; we, who do know sin, become the righteousness of God. God "made Christ sin" clearly implies more than that Christ was a human being. Some interpreters suggest that Christ was "made sin" in the sense that he was a sin offering. However, the victim used for a sin offering does not become sin. Others think that the expression is Pauline in origin. Then "made sin" could refer to Gal. 3:10–14. There, Paul says that Christ "becomes cursed" because of his death by crucifixion. Paul uses Deut. 21:23 to prove this point, an interpretation that he shares with other Jews in the first century. By coming under the curse of the law, Christ has made it possible for a sinful humanity to receive righteousness through faith.

Paul's assertion that in Christ we become the "righteousness of

God" is ambiguous. Is righteousness, which is an attribute of God and Christ, merely credited to humans, or does Paul mean that humans are somehow transformed so that they become righteous? Some theological traditions have understood Paul's justification language to refer to imputed righteousness; others, to transformation of the believer. This passage does not provide a solution. Paul is looking to the communal side of the reality of salvation. Paul sees the reality of salvation in Christ to be at stake in the behavior of the community. He asks the Corinthians to show the "righteousness of God" that has been made possible by Christ in a specific act of reconciliation. He himself is eager for such reconciliation (v. 3).

What tasks of reconciliation face our communities? There may be some obvious division within the community. Paul warns us not to become too complacent about such a state of affairs. We might tend to shrug off such a problem as "only human." Of course, our experience of human communities is always imperfect. But we often use that imperfection as an excuse not to attempt to solve a problem, to overcome some of the sinfulness in our own lives, or to try to change a larger situation of division and hostility. Then we might look at Paul's image of the apostle as an ambassador of God's reconciliation. Does that message, which is God's appeal to humanity, go forth from our churches?

## GOSPEL: MATTHEW 6:1-6, 16-21

The Matthean traditions come from a community with strong ties to its Jewish origins that was undergoing a crucial period of self-definition. Speaking of the Pharisees as "hypocrites" was not an accurate characterization of the piety of the Jewish community. Speaking in this way helped the Matthean community to draw its own boundaries over against Judaism. Such expressions reminded Christians that "their way" was to be preferred to that of their neighbors. These sayings also show a tendency toward exaggeration and comic portrayal that is evident in the parables and sayings of Jesus. Jesus often portrayed humanity in a comic vein as a challenge to the hearer to see that humans could really live in a way that reflected the rule of God.

Matt. 6:1 contrasts external piety with that which receives its reward from God. This introduction sets the theme for the section. The young Christian community would have to explain what made it different from the Jewish community. Matthew is not talking about an internal, private piety as superior to communal expressions of worship. Such a concept of private piety would never have occurred to anyone in the first century. All of one's behavior was public. Religion, whether a pagan sacrifice or Jewish worship in the synagogue, was equally a matter of public concern and community behavior. It affirmed the individual's place within the community.

Christians found themselves religiously isolated from their community of origin. For Gentile Christians, this separation was part of the process of conversion, since they could no longer participate in rites directed toward the pagan gods. For Jewish Christians, the separation was much more gradual. Matthew has reshaped traditions of Jesus that dealt with false piety to set Christianity over against the Jewish community. The sayings originally spoke of the radical discipleship demanded by the kingdom of God in which conventional standards of piety would no longer be sufficient. Matthew's introduction focuses our attention on the contrast between "us Christians" and the "Jews."

These verses describe the three pious practices of Judaism—almsgiving, prayer, and fasting. Christians are instructed to seek the reward that comes only from God. Matthew is not merely concerned to distinguish Christians from outsiders. Rather, some exegetes suggest, Matthew sees a danger from within his own community. He wishes to make sure that Christians and their leaders do not fall into the ostentatious and domineering posture of religious leaders and teachers that he has seen elsewhere. Thus, the criticism implied in the us/hypocrites contrast is aimed at Christians. They must not allow their religious practice to become corrupted by a false piety that prides itself in public display.

These sayings suggest a radical ethos of devotion to God that does not concern itself with reward in any way. The saying about giving alms presents the hearer with a deliberate paradox: one hand should not know what the other is doing. If you think that an easy feat, try learning to juggle. Separating the tosses of the left and right hands is the most difficult part of the whole process. We are so familiar with the injunction not to let the left hand know what the right hand is doing that we often forget its difficulty. And what about our concerns when giving alms? Seeing the peculiarity of the first saying enables us to see that the next two sayings are equally paradoxical. We are told not to pray in an obvious, public fashion—peculiar enough in antiquity—but to go into a storeroom to pray! How many of us would really take to the cellar or attic? When fasting, we are told to dress as though for a party. Fasting in "black tie and tails" is hardly what we would expect. This paradoxical and almost comic twist is typical of sayings and parables of Jesus. We need to appreciate the reorientation of our customary ways of behavior implied by this vision of the piety of the disciple. Matthew has understood that it serves as a warning to the Christian community not to fall into the trap of a religiosity that creates its own rewards for the pious, whether in public approval or in status and power over others based upon one's religious position.

As long as one even notices what one gives as alms, one is not acting out of real generosity. The Good Samaritan (Luke 10:29–37) is an example of such generosity. The Samaritan does not consider that the man is an enemy, nor does he spare any expense in taking care of him. We know well enough that our own efforts at charity fall far short of such generosity. Collecting contributions for charity usually requires special forms of acknowledgment and even some social pressure to give. This saying holds out a different image: charity that is so spontaneous that it does not even register from one hand to the next. We may all know a few people who could legitimately be said to fall into this category, but most of us have a long way to go.

The saying on prayer is more difficult for us to appreciate. We tend toward a certain embarrassment about public acts of prayer that is not typical of other cultures. In a society in which all acts of prayer, even those in the home, are public, this saying has quite an impact. As a public act, prayer or sacrifice to the gods ensured the good order of the society or family. If such rites were suddenly neglected, people would become extremely uneasy. In such a situation it is impossible to separate piety from social patterns of "good behavior." Jesus' saying challenges the disciples to see prayer as completely independent of that context. Strip it all away, and then see if a person still prays to the Lord. When we look at the saying from this perspective, it becomes evident that Jesus is not trying to eradicate public worship. He is challenging the way in which we engage in such worship.

While almsgiving and prayer are still part of our religious practice, fasting is less common. Many Americans also find it difficult to distinguish fasting from "going on a diet." We need to recover the sense of fasting as a great act of public worship that is evident in the Joel reading. Our fasting and self-denial during Lent is not aimed at "getting something." Yet we often choose our Lenten practice so that we can console ourselves with the benefit we will derive. Matthew saw that Jesus' sayings provided a challenge toward a different type of piety. The final sayings in vv. 19–21 are attached to those about piety by the notion of reward. These sayings are directed against preoccupation with wealth. Verses 19–20 present images of the fragility of our material possessions: woolen garments are eaten by moths; rust devours that new car, and thieves steal precious possessions. We are as preoccupied with protecting our possessions against such hazards. My cleaner promises to clean and store all my winter things; Rusty Jones, to take care that my car will not rust; and antitheft devices, to protect my property. What does such concern get us? Our consumer society makes this saying even more difficult to swallow. We are constantly encouraged to pile up possessions.

Verse 21 concludes with a proverb-like application: "where your treasure is, there will your heart be also." The injunction to "lay up treasure in heaven" does not reverse the earlier sayings about piety, as though one were to calculate the treasures being gained there. Rather, the orientation of a person's heart is a fundamental attribute of piety. The conflict between preoccupation with wealth and piety was raised often by religious teachers in Jesus' day. Matthew has turned that question on the Christian audience. We need to ask ourselves what it is that constitutes our treasure. To what do we really give our concern and attention? What do we really fear losing?

Matthew has taken Jesus' sayings about discipleship and piety as the core of the identity of the Christian community. The community is challenged to define itself in light of those sayings. Alms, prayer, and fasting must be directed toward God in a way that undercuts any human rewards, pressures, or motivation. We are always under God's judgment insofar as God sees and rewards what flows from true piety.

One should certainly not presume that God is a harsh judge piling up offenses by reading what is in our hearts. Just as Joel answered the question about the day of the Lord by proclaiming God's mercy, so the message of Jesus is one of compassion and mercy. But we can never presume on that compassion. These sayings warn that our lives as Christians are to be different from those of others. The sayings about where one's treasure is provide a striking example of such reorientation. If our lives as persons or as a community are dictated by the pressures and anxieties of the world or the needs generated by the constant blitz of advertising to which we are subject, then we can hardly say that our treasure lies in heaven. And we will certainly have to watch out that those attitudes do not corrupt our relationship with God.

## The First Sunday in Lent

| Lutheran | Roman Catholic | Episcopal | Pres/UCC/Chr | Meth/COCU |
|---|---|---|---|---|
| Gen. 22:1–18 | Gen. 9:8–15 | Gen. 9:8–17 | Gen. 9:8–15 | Gen. 9:8–17 |
| Rom. 8:31–39 | 1 Pet. 3:18–22 | 1 Pet. 3:18–22 | 1 Pet. 3:18–22 | 1 Pet. 3.18–22 |
| Mark 1:12–15 | Mark 1:12–15 | Mark 1:9–13 | Mark 1:12–15 | Mark 1:9–15 |

### FIRST LESSON: GENESIS 22:1–18

Abraham's sacrifice of Isaac has always been a challenge to the imagination. The story contains old traditions, which served various functions. One early stratum provided an etiology for the name of the mountain. Another tradition dealt with the substitution of animal sacrifice for the sacrifice of the eldest son. The mode of reflection that brought these stories of Abraham together developed a new understanding of God. Instead of speaking simply of God's favor leading to blessing or God's wrath leading to disaster, this story presents testing, which is neither blessing nor wrath. Verse 1 introduces the motif of divine testing. Testing is not to be identified with a psychological experience of being tempted. Abraham is not being tempted to engage in the Canaanite religious practice of child sacrifice. We know God's perspective on the story and on Abraham. The child in question is more than a firstborn son. Isaac is the child of promise, given to Abraham by God. The writer emphasizes the special character of Isaac with the expression, "your only son, whom you love." In the legal sense testing was a special rite or ordeal used to bring to light the guilt or innocence of an accused person (see Exod. 15:25b; 1 Kings 8:31). God has previously tested Abraham in calling him from Mesopotamia (12:1ff; 15:1ff). The famine in Gen. 12:10ff appears to be a test which Abraham did not pass. However, Abraham responds appropriately to the angelic visitors who announce Isaac's birth (18:1ff). This idea of testing can also be applied to the history of Israel (Deut. 13:3; Judg. 2:22). The image of Israel as the one tested by God is recapitulated in the stories of Jesus' faithfulness in divine testing.

Verses 2–8 give the details of the preparations and the journey, culminating in Isaac's question. Verses 9–14 describe the sacrifice ending with the etiological legend of how the place received its name. Verses 15–18 were added when the Abraham stories were brought together with the covenant traditions. They reaffirm the covenant with the promise that all the nations of the earth are to be blessed through Abraham's seed. Christians saw this promise fulfilled in Jesus.

The meticulous account of the preparations enables the audience to anticipate the agony of the journey. Biblical narrative is not concerned with explicit statements about the inner emotions of the characters. We are shown the cost as well as the faith required of Abraham in the details of the story. The tension built up in the story is expressed in Isaac's question.

Abraham's answer avoids stating what God has demanded directly, but it does tell the truth both because God provided Isaac and because, as an audience familiar with the story knows, God will provide the sacrifice to be offered on the mount. Detailed description carries the story right to the point of sacrifice. Abraham never hesitates in fulfilling the command of the Lord. Though the audience has been reminded in v. 8 that Abraham will find a sacrifice provided, the story makes it clear that he is not expecting or asking for a reprieve.

The successful results of the test are announced in the assertion that Abraham "fears God." We would gain a false sense of the piety of the OT if we thought that fear of God was based on a picture of God as one who punished people ruthlessly. Nor is fear of the Lord to be envisaged as an emotional reaction to divine mystery. Rather, the expression is used in the Old Testament for an attitude of obedience to God (Gen. 20:11; 42:18; 2 Kings 4:1; Isa. 11:2; Prov. 1:7; Job 1:1, 8). Abraham's obedience has been amply demonstrated in the details of his preparation. Abraham is allowed to substitute the ram by divine command. Thus, he continues to demonstrate his perfect obedience.

This tradition also contains the element of naming the place of sacrifice. A more famous example occurs in the story of Bethel read next Sunday. "All that has come down to us" here is a pun which once explained the name of the sacred place. It does not explain the name Moriah, which was a secondary identification of the place. According to 2 Chron. 3:1, Moriah referred to the Temple mountain in Jerusalem. At some point in the transmission of the story, the name of the sacred place was lost because the site had not become a famous shrine.

Verses 15–18 tie the story to the covenant tradition. Abraham's obedience and "fear of the Lord" are the basis of the blessings of the covenant. This version of the promise to Abraham is formulated in three parts: (1) the large number of his descendants; (2) their victory over enemies; (3) other nations will bless themselves by Abraham's descendants.

Other versions of the promises to Abraham omit the promise of victory (12:1–3; 13:14–16; 15:7, 18; 24:7; 26:3–4, 24). It would appear to have been formulated with the traditions of the conquest of the land in view.

In its present form, the story celebrates the faithful obedience of the patriarch as the source of all the blessings of the covenant. The harsh and apparently contradictory test in which God asks Abraham to sacrifice the child of the promise is met with "fear of the Lord." Abraham meticulously carries out each detail of the preparations. Abraham's faithfulness is answered by God's promise. This version of the promise is the only one in which the Lord is said to confirm it with a binding oath. The story turns on the theme of testing, fear of the Lord (– obedience), and great blessing. We often fall victim to a naive view of religion as the source of immediate blessings or gratification for the believer. This story reminds us that the experiences of faith and obedience also have their times of great trial. We sometimes allow our knowledge of the ending of the story to obscure the testing involved. There will always be someone who protests, "But of course Abraham knew that God wouldn't really ask him to kill Isaac." The introduction to the story attempts to make it clear that that is exactly what God has demanded as a test: Isaac, the only son, whom Abraham loved. But we may also look at the testing of Abraham as a risk on God's part. Abraham's obedience is fundamental to the blessings of the covenant.

Again, the necessity for the human response of faithful obedience is also something that we sometimes overlook. Indeed, much of the story of Israel is about disobedience and lack of fidelity. We may treat those episodes as "human nature." But what we fail to see is that the divine blessings also seek and even require faithfulness from the human side. Even with divine mercy and fidelity that go beyond what humans deserve, God has taken a risk on human freedom. Isaac is not only Abraham's beloved son, he is also the child of God's promise. That divine promise of salvation is not some miracle imposed from above. It is part of a relationship described in terms of covenant and of promises. And, since God does not compel humanity, the story is one with two sides. The human side is expressed in testing and obedience. Kierkegaard speaks of Abraham receiving Isaac from God a second time on Moriah. This description is a good one for the result of such a testing of faith. Abraham's faithful obedience makes the story of the people of God possible. God's own promise was placed at the risk of human obedience.

## SECOND LESSON: ROMANS 8:31–38

With Abraham we saw the beginning of the story of the promises of God to his people. With Jesus a new era of salvation is initiated. In biblical times, many people were looking forward to a new age of salvation in which humanity's persistent sinfulness would be eradicated. Some described it as the destruction of all evil followed by a new creation in which humanity and God would dwell together as though in paradise. Paul saw the death and resurrection of Jesus as the

"first fruits" of that transformation of all things. This passage concludes a description of that promise of "new creation" and its relationship to the Christian life. The opening series of questions (vv.
31–34) provides hints that Paul is not merely speculating about new
creation for the fun of it. He is speaking of experiences that might
seem to call the whole Christian promise of salvation into question.
This account of the new creation follows the famous discussion of the
law and human sinfulness in Romans 7. That chapter suggested that
the experience of humanity under the law/covenant had shown that
humans were unable to obtain the blessings of the covenant because
sin corrupted the purpose of the law. Paul perceives that as Messiah
Christ does not simply renew or intensify obedience to the law. Instead, Christ makes righteousness available to us as sinners apart
from the law. But it might still appear that the new age had not come
and hence that salvation remains for the future. Sin and disobedience
are still part of human experience, even of the experience of Christians. How can Christians speak about living in that new age if the
realities of sin and disobedience continue to be present? Paul will
insist that righteousness in Christ is more than sufficient precisely
because our imperfect human obedience is no longer the foundation of
our relationship with God.

Verses 31–34 open with legal metaphors. The prophetic tradition
had used legal metaphors to speak of God's lawsuit for breach of
covenant against a disobedient people. Paul will use a series of rhetorical questions to show that God is on the side of the Christian against
any possible condemnation that might be brought forward. One question after another presses this point home: "If God is for us, who is
against us?" (v. 31). This confidence is linked with the salvation that
has come through Christ. God would not spare the Son. God will
hardly fail to keep the promise to those who have been saved through
the Son's death. God offers his own Son. God does not demand the
sacrifice of some other person. People sometimes object that the
language of a sacrificial death of Jesus in order to save humanity is
barbaric. They are often thinking of God as a cruel and vindictive
tyrant who demands human sacrifice and suffering. Such an image of
God may tell us a great deal about the dynamics of the sinful human
psyche, but it does not reflect the God that we find in the biblical

stories. That God always acts with unexpected mercy, faithfulness, and kindness. Contrasted with the tale of human sinfulness in Romans 7, God's sacrifice of the Son is the epitome of love for humanity. Instead of seeing a human father sacrifice what is most precious to him, we see God make the sacrifice for us. Consequently, Paul argues, it would be absurd to suppose that God, who has suffered so much for us, would suddenly condemn.

Verses 33–34 make the legal metaphors more explicit. Who could possibly bring a charge against those who have been justified by God? Verse 34 answers the rhetorical question by affirming the creed of the early community. It contains a twofold formula proclaiming the death and resurrection of Jesus. This formula has been expanded with another early Christian tradition, that of Jesus' exaltation to the right hand of God. This exaltation tradition holds that Jesus serves as intercessor for Christians (see 1 John 2:1; Heb. 4:14–16; 8:1). He is our defense attorney in the heavenly court. Other examples of this tradition use it to address the problem of Christian sinfulness. Both 1 John and Hebrews see the exalted Jesus as a promise of mercy and forgiveness for Christians. This passage is similar. Any charges that might be brought are dismissed. Whatever our experiences of sinfulness and failure, they cannot negate the salvation that comes through faith.

Verses 35–39 turn to the love of God. Paul uses a list of trials and tribulations that might be suffered by the Christians to ask whether these might somehow separate us from Christ (v. 35). The catalogue of human and natural disasters is supplemented with a citation from Ps. 44:22 in v. 36. The person faithful to God is subject to persecution. Such persecution and hardship do not prove that God has rejected that person. This reference might well evoke the sufferings of Christians in the Roman community. Verse 37 brings the passage to its first conclusion. Christ's love makes it possible for the Christian to conquer such obstacles and more: "We are more than conquerors," Paul writes. God's love is the final motive for the confidence that Christians have in their salvation.

Verses 38–39 expand the theme of the previous verses. Paul substitutes for the earlier catalog of hardships a list of possible extremes that might separate us from Christ. These pairs represent the entire universe, "anything else in all creation." This list takes a cosmic perspective which goes well beyond the dimensions of human experience in the previous list. Anything that one might consider to come between us and God's promised salvation is overcome.

This passage offers us the opportunity to reflect upon the various circumstances that might erode our faith in God's salvation. Most of us may never consider the hidden questions about the love of God that are constantly raised in our experience. Notice that throughout this section the genitive refers to the love shown by Christ and by God. Paul is not concerned with the human side of loving God. We cannot claim to believe in the salvation that has been manifest in the death and resurrection of Jesus "for us" if we really believe that we live in the old creation in which our sinfulness is condemned, in which sufferings separate us from God, or in which the vastness and complexity of creation itself make God inaccessible.

Paul sees that our conviction that we are saved in Christ can be undermined by various charges that might be brought against this message of salvation. If we presume that humans are sinful, we may not see the possibility of bringing charges against the elect for their sinfulness as a challenge to belief with the sharpness that Paul does. We are perhaps more at home with the middle catalog of disasters. Personal suffering and persecution would seem to make the claim that God loves humanity difficult to believe. We still find ourselves suspicious of God in the face of suffering. Paul has shown us that in Christ God has taken on suffering to a degree that we could hardly imagine. We are victorious in suffering only because of that divine suffering.

Paul's list of cosmic factors also applies to our lives. We should consider whether our sense of the immensity of the cosmos; the threats of human destruction of the planet on which we live; the uncertainty of our own future, in which everything may be overturned by a disaster that we cannot control, do not play a role in reducing the confidence that we have in the promises of salvation held out by the gospel. Paul is suggesting to us an experience of salvation in which God's love overcomes all of these obstacles.

## GOSPEL: MARK 1:12–15

Mark does not report the nature of the temptation that Satan puts before Jesus in the wilderness. But, like the testing of Abraham, this temptation is initiated by divine agency. The Spirit, which Jesus received at his baptism, drives him to the wilderness. Jesus, we learn in the baptism scene, is God's beloved Son. As in the Abraham story, the author is not concerned with the psychological dimensions of temptation as an experience.

The wilderness plays a symbolic role in the Bible. The Exodus stories recount the testing of the people of God in the wilderness. In Jesus' time, some people expected that Israel would repeat that experience in the days before the coming of the new age. John the Baptist picked the wilderness as the place for his preaching. The Essene sect chose the desert near the Dead Sea as a location in which they, the faithful of Israel, would prepare the way for the coming of God. Thus, the picture of Jesus being driven into the wilderness by the Spirit of God for forty days of testing recapitulates the experience of the people of God. The Markan detail, "and he was with the wild animals," evokes a common motif from folklore. The holy person is one who can live with the wild animals unharmed. Such a person transcends the boundaries of creation as we experience it. Thus, this picture presents the wilderness as the paradisal place in which Jesus dwells, having overcome the temptation. The same theme is evident in the detail of the angels coming to minister to him.

The abrupt transition between the baptism and temptation scenes is repeated in the transition between the temptation and the beginning of Jesus' ministry. The relationship between Jesus' ministry and that of John the Baptist is not entirely clear. John 3:22–24 reflects a tradition that the two overlapped. Mark presumes that Jesus' ministry followed upon John's imprisonment. Mark does not recount the story of John's death in prison until 6:14–29. Mark 1:14–15 is the evangelist's transition to the story of the calling of the disciples which begins the narrative of Jesus' ministry (v. 16).

Mark's transitional verses make the ministry of Jesus the immediate consequence of his return from the wilderness. The message of repentance which Jesus announces is that of the Baptist. However, the announcement, "the time is fulfilled and the kingdom is at hand," (v. 15a) followed by the call to "repent and believe in the gospel" points to the preaching of the early Christian community. Mark 1:1 used "gospel" as a heading for the whole work as the news about Jesus Christ as Son of God. The baptismal story introduced that motif again

(v. 11). Mark may have seen the temptation as a demonstration of Jesus' faithful sonship. The juxtaposition of the temptation and the opening of Jesus' ministry with a call to repentance and faith points to a decisive intervention of God in salvation history. As in the prophetic traditions, the audience is reminded that time has run out. The day of the Lord is at hand. The only appropriate human response to such an announcement is to repent. The Christian preacher adds the special message that one must accept salvation in Christ. Mark uses v. 14 to shift the location of the ministry of Jesus from the wilderness around Jerusalem to Galilee. With the reference to "the gospel," Mark has concluded the introductory section of his work. The reader has seen that Jesus is the beloved Son of God, who was faithful in his testing. The story of the ministry of the Son of God is set to begin.

We tend to psychologize the story of the temptation in the desert as though we could somehow extrapolate from our own experience into the experience of Jesus. But the economy of the Markan narrative does not permit such expansion. Divine testing is, as we have already seen with Abraham, a special activity of the Spirit directed at the transitional figures in salvation history. Jesus is faithful where Israel was not. The wilderness has been transformed into the expected paradise. This symbolic picture belongs to the announcement that the kingdom of God is, indeed, at hand.

Two themes run through these readings: obedience under God's testing and the divine promises of a renewed creation or salvation. The readings also show us the ways in which faith transcends obstacles that stand in its way. Abraham responds to the divine command with faithful obedience. He experiences again the joy at receiving Isaac from God, and the promises of blessing are extended to his descendants and through them to all of humanity. Paul presents God's faithfulness and love in Jesus as the foundation of the salvation for a sinful humanity. Mark provides a brief glimpse of Jesus as the faithful, beloved Son. None of us would be so brash as to claim the faithful obedience that we see in Abraham or in Jesus. Our experiences of testing are much more like that of Israel during the forty years in the wilderness. Paul finds a basis for our salvation that does not depend upon our ability to become like Abraham or Jesus, even though their faithful obedience is certainly an example of what our relationship to

God should be. Christ's death "for us" is the source of our righteousness and salvation. We see the loving concern of God evident in the death and resurrection of Jesus. Such love cannot be negated by any form of opposition: by any of the sufferings and hardships of life; not even by any of the powers of the universe. We have seen the risk of human freedom that was associated with the covenant. The death and resurrection of the Son of God make it certain that nothing will ever come between God and the believer. Our Christian obedience and "fear of the Lord" are to flow from this vision of God's love for us.

# The Second Sunday in Lent

| Lutheran | Roman Catholic | Episcopal | Pres/UCC/Chr | Meth/COCU |
|---|---|---|---|---|
| Gen. 28:10–17 (18–22) | Gen. 22:1–2, 9, 10–13, 15–18 | Gen. 22:1–14 | Gen. 22:1–2, 9–13 | Gen. 28:10–22 or Gen. 22:1–18 |
| Rom. 5:1–11 | Rom. 8:31b–34 | Rom. 8:31–39 | Rom. 8:31–39 | Rom. 8:31–39 |
| Mark 8:31–38 | Mark 9:2–10 | Mark 8:31–38 | Mark 9:1–9 | Mark 8:31–38 |

### FIRST LESSON: GENESIS 28:10–22

Several stories of Jacob's encounters with the Lord are associated with cultic observances (see Gen. 32:2, 23–32; 35:1–7, 14–15). This tradition serves as an etiology for the great cult center at Bethel. Elements of surprise encounter and of the dangers of the journey pervade the story (vv. 10, 11, 16f). Jacob, having just received the blessing intended for his brother Esau (27:43–45), has been warned to flee. Although Jacob has gained his brother's blessing by a form of deceit, the narrative does not make the promise descend through such an act. The author uses this occasion to establish a covenant between God and Jacob.

Verses 10–12 show Jacob stopping to rest in a holy place. The name *Bethel* means *house of God*. In his dream, Jacob sees a great ramp, like the temple ziggurats of Mesopotamia. Angels descend and ascend upon the steps of this tower into the heavens. This vision marks the spot on which Jacob sleeps as the gateway into heaven. Much religious symbolism imagines the most holy places to be those at which heaven and earth touch. Thus, the cultic site at Bethel is imagined as being at the center of the cosmos. The angels serve as God's messengers, ascending and descending to fulfill divine commands and to oversee the activities of humans on earth.

Verses 13–15 interrupt the story of the sacred place with a second encounter. Jacob receives the promises of the covenant. This tradition was independent of the Bethel tradition as is evident from the fact that v. 16 resumes the theme of the holiness of the place without any reference to the covenant. The "God of the fathers," a title from the patriarchal period, is associated with the covenant promises in Gen. 26:24, 28:13; and 32:9. Since promises of the land are not appropriate to the patriarchal period, scholars think that this tradition was formulated when Israel was beginning to settle down in the land. This section identifies the God of the fathers with the Lord (v. 13). It also includes an unusual formulation of the promise of the land: Jacob is promised the land on which he lies, that is, Bethel and its environs.

Verse 15 is tied to Jacob's situation in the story, since he is promised that the Lord will be with him wherever he wanders and will bring him back to the land. The story incorporates the need for divine deliverance from the dangers of the journey into the format of a vow, which Jacob must fulfill. People settled in a land felt that their gods were tied with the homeland and its sacred places. Consequently, one of the dangers of a journey away from home or of exile was loss of the protection of one's gods. The experiences of exile would teach Israel the lesson reflected in this promise: God is not bound to a particular place, even one as holy as the sanctuary at Bethel.

Verses 16–17 return to the theme of the holy place. The site had once been used as a Canaanite sanctuary. At one point in its history, this story represented the cult of the Lord taking over that of a Canaanite deity. For those who heard this story while attending a religious festival at the great Israelite sanctuary, Jacob's words about the sacredness of the place pointed to their experience of worship. Taken with v. 15 one finds a dialectic between possession of the place and divine protection no matter where a person happens to be. That promise may have encouraged those who had come to the shrine on a pilgrimage that their own journey would be protected (1 Sam. 10:3; Judg. 20:18, 26–28; 21:2). The sanctuary appears to have been at its height during the tenth century when the traditions that make up the Genesis narrative were being formulated.

The story may once have ended with the unexpected discovery of a sacred place. The god who dwells in this intersection of heaven and earth turns out to be the God of the patriarch and of his fathers. For those more rooted in their ancestral place than Americans, one of the perils of journeying is the loss of the familiar landmarks and of the sacred places in which it was possible to contact the gods. Though we currently experience a spiritual fad for recounting one's life story as a ''journey,'' we have little appreciation of the risk and loss that accompany a journey. Wherever we go in the United States or Canada, we can count on the same fast food chains, movies, and TV shows. We all use the same brand-name products and watch carbon copies of the brand-name news filled in with local items. Thus, we are isolated from the real risks and surprises of journeying. Jacob's journey is under the protection of the Lord. He will be brought safely back to the place in which he has found God.

Verses 18–22 add another motif. Jacob makes a vow to the Lord; he also establishes Bethel as a great cult center. The stone which had formed his pillow is transformed into a great pillar. Sacred pillars found by archaeologists are often seven feet high. Some scholars think that the ritual at the sanctuary at Bethel included an opportunity for the participants to anoint the stone as Jacob had done. Jacob's vow includes three elements. If God protects him, he will take God as his god, he will establish a sanctuary at Bethel, and he will dedicate a tenth of all that he has to the Lord. Amos 4:4 refers to those who come bringing their tithes to the sanctuary. When Bethel was functioning as a sanctuary, the worshipers only had to look around them to see the fulfillment of the vow that Jacob had made. This sanctuary stood as evidence that the divine promises to the house of Jacob had been fulfilled. However, Amos warned against false confidence, which led the people to think that their elaborate worship and prosperity were signs of divine approval while they oppressed the poor and neglected the obligations of justice.

In antiquity a person would make a vow to a god or goddess to be paid if the deity delivered the worshiper from a particular danger. We might regard the vow as a rather primitive "bargain" with God. However, people today in periods of stress often make such promises to God with much less sense of the obligation to fulfill the vow than our ancestors had. The pattern of the covenant promises structured the faith of Israel around the obligations of the covenant as a response for the benefits that God had already bestowed. Here, allegiance to the Lord, worship at the sacred shrine, and payment of tithes are all established as the response owed God for keeping the patriarch safe.

Sometimes we think only of obligations that God has toward us. Persons might say, for example, that they no longer attend church because they do not like the service or the sermons. Such persons are presuming that worship is for ourselves, rather than for God in thanksgiving for our lives and prosperity. Tithing presumes that part of that prosperity should also be returned to God. We may ask whether we have any sense of obligation to use our material wealth for any purposes other than our own immediate desires. If we do not, then we are inferior to the Bible in understanding the obligations of property and prosperity.

## SECOND LESSON: ROMANS 5:1–11

For Paul, the greatest sign of God's graciousness toward humanity is the death of Christ. Christians must respond to the divine initiative. Paul constantly emphasizes the fact that we do not earn reconciliation. In the opening verses, the life of the Christian is qualified by the new situation in Christ: justified by faith means peace with God, access to grace, and rejoicing in the hope of sharing the glory of God. Hope implies that the Christian evaluates his or her present experience in a special way. This special insight is made clear in a chain of virtues which Paul uses to work out the implications of hope (vv. 3–5). We boast, Paul says, in tribulations because tribulation produces endurance, which in turn produces proven character, which leads to hope. Christians can also be sure that their hope will not be in vain because of God's love. The evidence of God's love for us is the Holy Spirit, which God has given to the believer.

The second half of the passage turns to the death of Christ. Paul emphasizes the fact that we are made righteous as sinners. Our peace with God is not something earned through our own virtue. Christ did not die for a humanity that was obedient to the covenant but for one which was sinful. Precisely because Christ died for a sinful humanity, the reconciliation with God that flows from his death is "once for all." It is not an offer that is contingent upon human repentance and conversion in order to take effect. According to Paul, the history of humanity had shown a fatal connection with sinfulness that made such offers unworkable. For the Christian the "once for all" character of the death of Christ guarantees that nothing can come between the believer and the hope of sharing divine glory.

Both justification and reconciliation imply that the believer is saved from the wrath of God that is to come upon a sinful humanity (5:9a). We are not to think of the death of Christ as a payoff to a wrathful God. The presence of the risen Jesus with God is the guarantee of our salvation. Justification evokes the overtones of our fulfilling that righteousness which God had intended for humanity as shown in the law. Reconciliation carries other overtones that were important in Paul's ministry. While the Jews were God's people, the Gentiles were often perceived as God's enemies, since they worshiped false gods. Paul sees in Christ the coming of a new people of God in which the Jew and Gentile are both "made righteous" through their faith in Christ. Thus, the division between the two is broken down. Paul can even speak of the apostolic ministry as a ministry of reconciliation (2 Cor. 5:17–21). Paul has insisted that this message of reconciliation is to be preached to humanity as a whole. Thus, it plays an important role in defining the task of the Christian mission.

It is difficult to draw sharp lines between the past event of salvation, the present life of the believer, and the future for which one hopes. Exegetes sometimes try to systematize Paul's thought in stages: (1) justification as the Christ-event appropriated in faith; (2) sanctification, the transforming operation of justification in the heart of the believer; (3) salvation as the future share in the glory of God. Paul never claims that we attain all the benefits of salvation now. There is still a future to salvation, which the believer could lose.

But a decisive break lies between the past in which we were sinners and our present as those who have been made righteous. An important element of the Christian life is the Christian's ability to recall the past action of God as present in the experience of suffering. Christians know that in their suffering the saving power of God that was manifest in the crucifixion is also present. When the Christian speaks of being saved from the coming wrath of God, he or she looks to the vindication of Christ in his exaltation at God's right hand. God's faithfulness in raising Christ from the dead will be matched in the future glory given to all those who have received righteousness as a free gift through faith in Christ.

Both sections of this passage contain the exhortation to rejoice. One rejoices in present sufferings because of the knowledge of what they produce. Nor is the positive side of salvation entirely located in the future, since the Christian experiences the love of God. Paul concludes with the reminder that the Christian finally rejoices in God from whom all salvation comes. Paul's orientation toward the future is not, then, simply asserting that suffering will end in glory. Righteousness, reconciliation with God, and the gift of the Spirit are all present realities. The categories of salvation cut across the temporal lines that separate past, present, and future without distinguishing the difference between them. The past is the point at which humans are sinners, separated from God and all deserving of condemnation in the judgment. Christ's death has made righteousness and salvation possible for those who believe. The believers experience the reality of that love of God and righteousness in their life. Their endurance in sufferings shows the confidence and character that they possess. Thus, Christians do not need great theophanies like Jacob's to tell us that we stand in a holy place. In Christ God has chosen and reached out to the believer, who can enjoy the blessings of being at peace with God. Both the story of Jacob and Paul's exhortation remind us that human beings must make an appropriate response to the salvation received from God. Jacob establishes the sanctuary and dedicates part of his property to God. Paul encourages the Christian to rejoice confidently in tribulation. Such rejoicing acknowledges the love of God that has been shown in Christ.

### GOSPEL: MARK 8:31–38

Mark links Jesus' suffering with the need for his disciples to reevaluate their own understanding of suffering. We often think that the real acts of God are those in which God appears in a powerful or dramatic way. Some of Jesus' contemporaries looked for God to provide them with a powerful leader who would overthrow their enemies, purify worship at the Temple, and make Israel the exemplary people of God. Whatever expectations may have been raised by Jesus' miracles and preaching, his ministry cannot be said to have met those expectations. Mark situates this passage between two affirmations that Jesus is the expected Messiah, Peter's confession, and the transfiguration. Jesus' messiahship is to be different from the expectations of power and glory held up by the people.

The first part of the passage emphasizes that it is God's plan for the Son of man to suffer (vv. 31–34). The second part instructs Jesus' disciples about how they are to follow such a Messiah. The two sections are separated by a shift in audience. The revelation of Jesus' messianic suffering is addressed only to the group of Jesus' disciples. They were told not to tell others that Jesus is Messiah. The section on discipleship is addressed to all of those gathered to hear Jesus. Mark consistently portrays Jesus' disciples as struggling and failing to understand his teaching about suffering. This passage contains the first of three predictions of the passion (also 9:30–32; 10:32–34). In each case Mark makes the description of the fate that awaits Jesus more explicit and increases the misunderstanding of the disciples. In each case a lesson about what it means to be the disciple of a Messiah like Jesus follows the passion prediction. The lessons of discipleship in chapters 9 and 10 are provoked by false understandings of what greatness means. In our passage Peter's reaction to the passion prediction provokes the lesson about discipleship.

Mark 8:31 has been shaped by the early Christian identification of the risen and exalted Jesus with the Son of man figure in Dan. 7:14ff. There, "one like a son of man" ascends to the divine throne and assumes sovereignty over the nations. Use of such an image in a passion prediction heightens the paradox of a Messiah who is to be crucified and rejected by the people. The suffering and death of the Messiah is part of God's plan of salvation and not merely another accident of human sinfulness. Christians filled out their understanding of the passion as part of salvation history with passages from the OT that referred to the suffering of the righteous person.

Peter reacts by rebuking Jesus. This word *epitimao* appears in v. 30, where the disciples are told not to reveal that Jesus is the Messiah. It also can be addressed to demons in exorcism (see 1:25). Peter's rebuke to Jesus will be followed by Jesus' rebuke to him (v. 33). There the force of the exorcism is apparent, since Peter is addressed as "Satan." Thus, vv. 30–33 are linked together by the increasingly sharp elements of rebuke. The culmination lies in the words addressed to Peter, "You do not think the things of God but those of human beings." The issue is the contrast between a human understanding of what it means to be Messiah and the understanding of God that is represented in the prediction of the suffering Son of man.

Our familiarity with Jesus' suffering should not lead us to presume that we are superior to Peter. We often presume that God should exercise divine power to deal with evil. We rarely think of God as one who suffers. We may even associate Jesus more directly with the divine power of the miracles or the coming of judgment than we do with the suffering of the cross. We may treat the cross as merely a human mistake or a sign of the perversity of evil in that the religious leaders of the people can reject God's Messiah. It is all too easy to let the cross be overridden by the images of Christ exalted with the Father as a triumphant victor over his enemies.

The contrast between the divine and human way of thinking carries over into the sayings on discipleship. The disciple cannot expect a fate different from that of Jesus. This passage is made up of a series of independent sayings of Jesus. Matthew locates them in a discourse directed toward the disciples whom Jesus sends out on a mission (Matt. 10:33, 38, 39). The Lukan parallels are scattered around in the Gospels (e.g., Mark 8:38||Luke 12:9; Mark 8:35||Luke 17:33; Mark 8:34||Luke 14:27), where they serve as general exhortations to discipleship. A variant of Mark 8:35 has also found its way into the tradition in John 12:25. John 12:26 contains a distant echo of Mark 8:34. Thus, the connection between these discipleship sayings and the passion of Jesus antedates both Gospels.

The first saying draws an explicit parallel between Jesus' fate and discipleship (v. 34). Matt. 10:37 and Luke 14:26 introduce this saying with a tradition about hating family and even one's own self in order to follow Jesus. They suggest that an early interpretation of "deny self" meant rejecting all of those ties that might hold a person back from following Jesus.

The saying about losing one's life in order to save it (v. 35) follows

the pattern of eschatological reversal. In the messianic age the
wealthy and powerful people of this world will find themselves of no
account, while the poor and powerless will be exalted. The context of
the saying leaves no doubt about its eschatological character, since it
is followed by predictions about the coming of the Son of man in
judgment. We see that judgment is exercised according to the standard
set by the suffering Son of man. The combination of the exalted Son of
man, who judges the nations, with the suffering Son of man of the
passion defines the life of the Christian. Two rhetorical questions
serve to underline the significance of this perspective (vv. 36–37).
They also provide an interpretation of what is meant by preserving
one's life. They challenge the attempt to preserve oneself by gaining
wealth. Parallel reflections also appear in wisdom traditions which
point to the futility of such human projects (see Ps. 49:5–9). The
tradition questions the false human confidence in wealth. At the same
time, it lays bare the driving force behind the frantic desire to acquire
riches, the presumption that one can somehow protect one's life from
death. Mark's questions evoke that tradition for the audience. Its
warning is now applied to those persons who might hesitate to follow
Jesus. What do they think that they are protecting that makes them
afraid of following him?

Verse 38 brings the challenge of discipleship forward as a warning.
It suggests that Christians faced situations in which some might even
be tempted to deny Jesus, perhaps in the context of persecution (see
Mark 13:9–13). Mark 8:38 warns that those who deny Jesus will find
themselves condemned in the judgment. The variant in Matt. 10:33
leaves out the apocalyptic description of the present as an "adulterous
and sinful generation" and the apocalyptic description of the Son of
man coming in the glory of the Father with his angels. Instead, the
image evoked is one of Jesus with the Father in the heavenly court.
There Jesus will refuse to acknowledge the disciple who has denied
him "before human beings." Matthew appears to have made a general warning to Christian missionaries who might be tempted to slack
off in their testimony from the apocalyptic saying about those who
deny Jesus in face of the persecution of the last times. The warning
implied in the saying is an uncompromising one. Those who deny
Jesus will find themselves condemned.

Jesus' rebuke of Peter for thinking according to human standards rather than God's, the exposition of the cost of discipleship, and the warning about denying Jesus all introduce a sobering note into the reflection on divine grace that we find in the earlier readings. We have a difficult time not dividing our image of God into either/or categories. Either we think of God as a strict judge, or we presume that the salvation offered sinners will certainly cover the undramatic sins that are typical of most of our lives. But these readings show us that it is necessary to be careful in such quick evaluations. The Jacob story insists upon acknowledgment of the salvation and protection that one receives from God. Paul's emphasis on the salvation gained for sinners through the death of Christ presumes that the Christian no longer lives in the "sinful age" but out of the power of the Spirit. A person must respond accordingly. This response in both Paul and Mark places the Christian in a different position with regard to suffering than a person who is not Christian. The Christian can find a divine plan or purpose to suffering that is based in his or her expectation of salvation.

Mark's section on suffering and discipleship raises a challenge to the Christian. The disciple must be at God's disposal in the same way that Jesus is. One of the most difficult aspects of this Christian view is the challenge to break down the patterns of thinking that we have built up on the basis of other values. We all have devices by which we are seeking—often without realizing it—to protect our lives or ourselves. These strategies may involve attachment to material possessions, or they may involve our relationships with other people. The person who will keep everything under his or her control, who will seek to dominate every situation, is protecting a self that will ultimately be lost. These readings present us with a series of challenges during Lent. Are we responding with thanksgiving and rejoicing to the graciousness of God? Are we trying to use false ways of protecting ourselves that are undermining and corrupting our faith?

# The Third Sunday in Lent

| Lutheran | Roman Catholic | Episcopal | Pres/UCC/Chr | Meth/COCU |
|---|---|---|---|---|
| Exod. 20:1–17 | Exod. 20:1–17 or Exod. 20:1–3, 7–8, 12–17 | Exod. 20:1–17 | Exod. 20:1–3, 7–8, 12–17 | Exod. 20:1–17 |
| 1 Cor. 1:22–25 | 1 Cor. 1:22–25 | Rom. 7:13–25 | 1 Cor. 1:22–25 | 1 Cor. 1:22–25 |
| John 2:13–22 | John 2:13–25 | John 2:13–22 | John 2:13–25 | John 2:13–25 |

### FIRST LESSON: EXODUS 20:1–17

This account of the ten "words" which God addresses to the people is situated between two powerful appearances of the Lord. In Exod. 19:16–25 the Lord appears on Sinai like a blazing fire. No one, not even the priests, can touch the mountain without dying. In Exod. 20:18–20 the people become so frightened that they ask Moses to speak to them instead of God. Moses replies that God has come so that "fear of him may be before your eyes, that you may not sin." Thus, these words of the Lord are backed up with the full power of divine presence.

Exod. 20:1 links the Decalogue to the previous theophany. Verse 2 presents the commandments as the direct word of the Lord to the people. Deut. 5:4–21 has Moses remind the people of this scene. There it is interpreted as the foundation of a covenant which the Lord has made directly with the wilderness generation. Both versions contain the shorter explanations of the commandments. They differ in their account of the Sabbath legislation. Deuteronomy attaches it to the deliverance of the people from Egypt, while Exodus refers back to the Priestly account of creation (cf. Exod. 20:11 and Deut. 5:14b–15). The various traditions differ in how the commandments are divided into ten. Greek Orthodox and Reformed traditions begin the list with v. 3. The Roman Catholic and Lutheran traditions treat vv. 3–6 as a single commandment and divide verse 17 into two commandments. Jewish tradition divides the commandments into lists of short commandments:

(1) I, the Lord, am your God.
(2) Thou shalt have no other gods in my presence.
(3) Thou shalt not use the Lord's name perversely.
(4) Remember the Sabbath Day. Keep it holy.
(5) Respect thy father and mother.
(6) Thou shalt not kill.
(7) Thou shalt not commit adultery.
(8) Thou shalt not steal.
(9) Thou shalt not give false evidence.
(10) Thou shalt not covet.

The commandments are formulated as apodictic law. They are stated as absolute prohibitions without any attached conditions.

The Lord is identified as the God of the Exodus (v. 2). The "I am the Lord" formula appears in the Priestly tradition of the holiness code (Lev. 17–26). Ps. 50.7 uses the formula in the context of a legal suit by God against the people for lack of faithfulness to the covenant. Thus, the Decalogue opens by recalling to the people the fact of their deliverance. Obedience to the commandments which follow is to be rooted in the relationship which God has already established with the people.

Verses 3–6 demand exclusive worship of the Lord. "Before me" means in God's presence. Thus, the first of these commandments refers to an exclusive monotheism. The people are not to set up any other gods in the Lord's presence (cf. Deut. 6:14f). This commandment does not concern the reality of other gods. It states that there are to be no other gods in the cult of Yahwism. The prohibition of idols also concerns monolatry. The Lord's "jealousy" is the reason given for the prohibition. God has a passionate desire to belong to the people. The prophets will engage in explicit polemic against the idols of other peoples (Hos. 8:5; Isa. 44:9ff; Jer. 10). Scholars are divided over the question of whether or not there were idols which represented Yahweh in Israel. The cult itself was clearly imageless. The calves attributed to Jeroboam in 1 Kings 12:28–33 use the iconography of the Canaanite storm god to represent Yahweh. Some scholars argue that there may have been representations of Yahweh on the popular level. Here the prohibition of idols is tied to the rejection of other gods. Verse 5 makes that connection more explicit in prohibiting worship of any idol. It is also possible that the prohibition of idols was directed at the belief that an image of a god provided people with some form of power over that god. Verses 5 and 6 expand the demand for monolatry with reference to the Lord as a jealous God, who will not tolerate anything short of exclusive obedience. Love of God implies keeping God's commandments (cf. Deut. 6:5), and hating God implies disobedience. The threat of punishment for iniquity and the promise of steadfast love for those who are obedient would derive from the rewards and blessings of the covenant tradition.

The next command (v. 7) protects the name of God against misuse. Taking the name of God in vain refers to misusing it in curses, oaths, or sorcery. This prohibition may also be based on the feeling that there is some connection between the name and the one who bears it. The name "Yahweh" opens the passage. It is revealed to humanity for the purposes of worship. This prohibition concludes those commandments which deal with worship.

The Sabbath commandment makes the transition between the demands for monolatry and the commands which deal with the perversions of human relationships (vv. 8–11). Though the Sabbath is declared holy, the passage does not make any specific cultic provisions for the Sabbath. The holiness of the Sabbath is represented by the difference between it and the other days. Amos 8:5 and 2 Kings 4:23 attest to the fact that the Sabbath is a day on which no work or business can be conducted. While Exodus gives the Priestly code's reason for the Sabbath observance—it is the day on which God rested—Deut. 5:13–14 points to the deliverance from Egypt as the grounds for the Sabbath in concern for others who are enslaved. Both explanations are clearly secondary. The Sabbath command was to be inclusive. It included slaves, animals, and strangers living within the confines of Israel.

The remaining commandments deal with relationships between humans. The command to honor father and mother (v. 12) is expanded with the promise of long life in the land. This promise correlates with the command that is directed to adult children. They are to respect and care for aging parents (cf. Prov. 19:26; 20:20).

The prohibition against killing includes both premeditated and unintended killing, that is, all forms of illegal violence which cost another person's life. It does not prohibit legitimate execution of a criminal or the killing of enemies in war. The command against committing adultery would have included persons who were betrothed.

No object is given in the command against stealing. Since the commands so far have dealt with persons rather than with property, some scholars think that it referred to the stealing of persons. One finds the issue of stealing humans in Gen. 40:15. One was not to enslave a free Israelite.

The prohibition against false witness applies to testimony offered in legal situations. Prov. 19:9 links that false witness and lying. The legal business of the primitive agricultural community was conducted by the elders at the city gate. The proceedings would have been dependent upon the testimony of the various witnesses to agreements between parties.

Though we think of coveting as an inner state, the Hebrew word is regularly found in contexts which speak of stealing or taking another person's property violently. Thus the prohibition against coveting does not refer to a mental act but to any sort of violence by which one might attempt to gain another's property.

These words of the Lord set forth the conditions of the covenant society. It is to be completely devoted to the worship of the God who has brought the people out of Egypt. The day of Sabbath rest apparently reflects a unique social institution in Israel. The remaining prohibitions regulate the fundamental relationships between persons in any society. Although scholars are not certain about the age of the Decalogue tradition, Hos. 4:2 presupposes that it is known. The foundational character of these commands makes them as applicable to later societies as to the Israelite society. The Decalogue continues to be a guide to those relationships which are pleasing to God. All human communities must deal with the problems that are implicit in the second half of the Decalogue: treatment of the aged; illegal violence against persons; adultery; stealing, or, in different forms, the enslavement of some persons in a society by others; false testimony, and the attempts of some to gain the possessions of others by violence or other machinations. Thus the commandments stand as a challenge to any society.

## SECOND LESSON: 1 CORINTHIANS 1:22-25

These verses conclude a section that began with v. 18, "The word *(logos)* of the cross is foolishness to those who are perishing, but to us who are being saved it is the power of God." Divisions have been created in the community by those who are concerned with the special gifts of the various apostles, including persuasive, elegant speech. Paul is attacking these human criteria of wisdom as contrary to the wisdom of God, which is demonstrated in the cross. One cannot make the case for belief in the cross according to human standards. God's wisdom and human wisdom are not commensurable. Paul pictures the folly of the cross as dividing humanity into two groups: those who are perishing and those who are being saved.

The division Jew/Greek encompasses all of humanity for Paul. The Jews are condemned for demanding signs. Such a demand represents a fundamental lack of trust in God, since it requires that God prove himself to humans (see Num. 14:11f). Demands for such authenticating signs were addressed to Jesus (see Mark 8:11 par.). Greeks, on the other hand, are preoccupied with wisdom. This concern for wisdom dominates much of the opening part of this letter. Both attitudes reflect the human claim to set standards by which God's action is to be evaluated. Paul seeks to confront this human demand with the truth of the cross as God's saving power.

The contrast of divine and human wisdom is linked with another which appears frequently in Paul, the contrast of power and weakness. The power of God is shown in weakness. The cross represents the power and wisdom of God (v. 24). Paul speaks of the division in humanity as created by the message itself. He does not suggest that some special form of preaching will turn the scandal and folly of the cross into something other than it is. Nor is the faith that sees the truth about the cross a human accomplishment. Paul describes the Christians as those who are "called." Thus, he presents their belief as based on God's own action. Verse 25 expands verse 24b as a general axiom, "The foolishness of God is wiser than humans, and the weakness of God is stronger than humans." This paradoxical formulation also implies that the activity of God never confronts humans with the type of persuasive force that we demand. It is not presented with overwhelming power or signs. Nor is it the subject of irrefutable logical demonstration or persuasive rhetoric.

Paul turns to a concrete application of the contrast in vv. 26ff. There he points to the Corinthians themselves. He reminds them that they cannot make claims to wisdom or power in the human sense. Yet they know from their own experience that God has called them to have faith. Therefore, God must not be concerned with those human criteria. Their own status demonstrates the truth of the axiom which Paul has formulated. If wisdom or power were the criteria of God's calling, then the Corinthians, who make so much of these things, could hardly expect to be among the elect. Since many people in antiquity presumed that a person's standing in the larger society also reflected that person's relationship with the gods, Paul's point about status, power, and wisdom would speak more forcefully to the Corinthians than it might to Americans. Recent studies of Paul's Corinthian church have suggested that it was comprised of a group of persons whose talents, ambition, and wealth led them to have a higher achieved status than that attributed to them on the basis of their origins and social class. It has been suggested that the paradox of the cross spoke to their experiences of "status inconsistency." At the same time, it would also appear that some of the turmoil in the Corinthian church was caused by those persons who attempted to wield the kind of power and influence within the Christian sphere that they could not exercise within the larger community. They may have looked at Christianity as a source of "wisdom and power" for the elect. Paul has taken great pains to destroy that mentality.

Paul is not declaring that one believes in the cross because of its paradox. Nor does he deny that the cross has its own wisdom (1 Cor. 2:6). But he consistently refuses to allow the message of the cross to be confused with a religion that promises the faithful miraculous powers or with a wisdom which would pass as profound in the human sense. We still find that people fall into one of these two traps. Sometimes it is the presumption that faith cures all the ills of life. Sometimes it is the presumption that the believer has a wisdom from the Bible, which knows everything that the sciences or other learned disciplines have discovered. Neither view is correct. Paul sees that Christian life involves the paradox of rejoicing in suffering. The wisdom of God to which he refers the believer is not human wisdom written larger. It is the wisdom of God's salvation through the cross, through what is apparently weak and foolish.

## GOSPEL: JOHN 2:13-22 (23-25)

The episode of the cleansing of the Temple occurs in the synoptic tradition at the end of Jesus' ministry (Mark 11:15–19 par.). The synoptic Gospels have Jesus visit Jerusalem only once, while the Fourth Gospel refers to several passover visits there. An alternating pattern of Galilee, then Jerusalem, dominates the first seven chapters of the Gospel. While many scholars find the tradition of a ministry that extended over several years and included earlier visits to Jerusalem historically plausible, the Temple incident may have been relocated from the passion tradition by the evangelist. He will use the story of the healing of Lazarus as the immediate occasion for the official decision to crucify Jesus (John 11:45–53).

This passage consists of two separate traditions, the Temple cleansing and the saying about the destruction of the Temple. The latter appears in the synoptics as part of the accusation by Jesus' enemies (Mark 14:58||Matt. 26:61; Mark 15:29||Matt. 27:40; also Acts 6:14). Thus, some scholars suggest that that saying belongs to an earlier period in Jesus' ministry. The episode of the cleansing of the Temple was a further prophetic action, which precipitated events leading to Jesus' death.

Common features in the synoptic and Johannine versions of the cleansing of the Temple include driving out the dove sellers, overturning the tables of the money changers, and reference to the Temple as God's house. The Johannine tradition is unique in including cattle, the making of a whip, and in the words attributed to Jesus. Since the citation from Ps. 69:9–10 occurs elsewhere as a testimony to Jesus (Rom. 15:3; Heb. 11:26), John has probably adopted the psalm to this occasion. The Johannine tradition also has a confrontation between Jesus and the Jewish authorities occur immediately, while the synoptic tradition separates the challenge from this incident.

The action itself is cast as a prophetic critique of the corruption of the Temple. In the synoptic traditions Isa. 56:7 and Jer. 7:11 are the basis for the words of Jesus. Exegetes find an allusion to Zech. 14:21 in

John 2:16. Zechariah's critique of the postexilic Temple and its priesthood was incorporated into other apocalyptic traditions of first century Judaism. Ezekiel 40—46 envisages the coming of a new Temple. Such expectations of a new Temple in the messianic age make the association between Jesus' saying about the Temple and the prophetic sign of cleansing the Temple a natural one.

The Johannine tradition originated in a community which was hostile to the Temple and which had experienced persecution by Jewish religious authorities. The incident shows that the authority of Jesus sets one on a collision course with the religious authority of Judaism. Within the Gospel, much of the conflict with Judaism is centered on the identity of Jesus and the Father. Jesus does not defend his teaching in terms acceptable to Jewish religious authorities. He points instead to the mission that he has received from the Father. One quickly sees that to reject Jesus' word is to reject the Word of God. John makes the citation of Ps. 69:9 something which the disciples "remembered." One learns in v. 22 that "remembering" has a technical sense for the Johannine community. It refers to the interpretation of Jesus in light of the Scripture, which occurred after Jesus' resurrection.

The challenge to Jesus' authority in vv. 18–20 parallels the requests for a sign in the synoptic tradition. Matt. 12:38–40 answers that request with a reference to the sign of Jonah interpreted as a type of Jesus' resurrection. The Johannine version of the Temple saying also contains a veiled reference to resurrection, since Jesus speaks of "raising up" rather than "building up" the Temple as in the synoptics. John uses such symbolic meanings throughout the Gospel. The questioners, who read Jesus' saying on a literal level, can only be perplexed. They interpret "build up" and "raise up" as synonyms (v. 20). However, the evangelist provides the reader with the understanding of the saying that the Johannine community had reached. They understood Jesus to be referring to his own body (v. 21). This postresurrection perception of the truth of Jesus' words is represented as belief in the Scripture and in Jesus' saying. Exegetes point out that this passage is an explicit example of the authority of a saying of Jesus being paralleled with that of Scripture. The clash between Jesus' word as the authoritative guide to the significance of Scripture and the claims of Jewish authorities about the meaning of what Moses revealed is another theme that will recur frequently in the Gospel.

The conclusion of the chapter (vv. 23–25) warns against a false faith based upon Jesus' signs (= miracles). For John, the only key to the truth about Jesus is the identity between Jesus and the Father. Unless Jesus' signs enable a person to see the glory of God in Jesus, the faith that they generate is worthless. Chapter 2 provides examples of three possible reactions to Jesus. The miracle at Cana enabled Jesus' disciples to see Jesus' glory and believe (v. 11). The belief in Jesus' word and the Scripture that leads the disciples to perceive that Jesus was speaking of his body is another example of the true faith of the disciples (vv. 17, 21f). On the other extreme, we find the open hostility of the authorities, "the Jews" (v. 18). They will not be able to see the truth of Jesus' words, since they are unable to see the truth that is implied in his answer.

Between Jesus' disciples and the hostile authorities stand the crowds who are attracted by Jesus' signs. We are warned that their faith is not reliable. Exegetes are not certain about how much weight should be placed on the comment that Jesus did not entrust himself to them. Perhaps this formulation of the story came from the period of persecution by Jewish authorities in which Johannine Christians found that some who had been Christians chose to remain within the Jewish community rather than suffer and hence rejected their faith in Jesus. Several incidents in the Gospel refer to such "cryptobelievers" (see 6:66; 9:22f; 12:42f). The Gospel also uses the theme of Jesus' knowledge and control of all things in connection with the passion. The reader is never allowed to think that the crucifixion represents the victory of Jesus' enemies or of Satan over the Son of God. The passage tells the reader that Jesus knew from the outset that many of those who followed him would not be true believers.

The readings give us three quite different examples of the divine Word. The words of the Decalogue provide the fundamental pattern for the community that is to live under God. However, both NT readings reflect the ways in which humanity has failed to live by the Word of God. For Paul, God's new Word to humanity is the message of salvation in the cross. But that Word is even less suited to human demands for power and wisdom than the words of the Decalogue.

Only those chosen ones who are able to hear with faith get past the stumbling block that the cross sets up. Human standards of power and wisdom will not help us to evaluate the Word of God.

The Johannine story refers back to the prophetic critique of the temple and its worship. The paradox, for John, is not simply the cross but Jesus' own presence as the one sent from the Father. Jesus cannot offer the religious authorities the type of sign that they would require. Instead, he refers to the sign of his own resurrection in fulfillment of the Scriptures. We are presented with three possible responses to the Word of God: the believer accepts that Word; the authorities for whom the word of Jesus appears to be nonsense reject it; and the crowd's unreliable response is based on the signs that Jesus does. A similar lack of trust may be evident in the Corinthian Christians, who looked to Christianity for power and wisdom that would count for something by human standards.

The question for most Christians is whether we find ourselves with the faith that is trustworthy or with a faith that is marred by the flaws reflected in the readings. As individuals we may feel that we measure up well against the Decalogue. But the Decalogue is addressed to the people as a whole. We are less confident that our communities are places in which such relationships obtain. Yet we may not even concern ourselves with making them better.

And what about Paul's questions? Do we, in fact, look to the paradox of power in weakness displayed in the cross? Or do we expect our religion to conform to the human standards of power and wisdom set by our society, just as the Corinthians looked toward those of their society? The persistent critique of the religious establishment by the prophets and then by Jesus warns of a similar danger. Though we may be more at home with concern for the social legislation of the Decalogue, the prophetic tradition sees that one cannot ignore the question of appropriate worship of God. It is possible for idolatrous worship to express itself in different forms: a temple concerned with the external trappings of worship rather than with being a place of prayer and a sign of God's presence with a people or the behavior of those of whom Amos spoke, who could hardly wait for the Sabbath to be over so that they could return to getting rich by defrauding people and charging unjust prices. If we look to religion for powers to cure the ills of our lives but not as something owed back to God, then we are looking for power and wisdom of the human sort, not of God's. If we can hardly wait to be done with religion so that we can get back to what really matters to us, the pursuit of wealth or some other personal goal, then we are as much idolaters as those who worship other gods. The conversion of heart during Lent seeks to transform such faltering faith into that which can be trusted.

## The Fourth Sunday in Lent

| Lutheran | Roman Catholic | Episcopal | Pres/UCC/Chr | Meth/COCU |
|----------|----------------|-----------|--------------|-----------|
| Num. 21:4–9 | 2 Chron. 36: 14–17, 19–23 | 2 Chron. 36: 14–23 | 2 Chron. 36: 14–21 | 2 Chron. 36: 14–23 |
| Eph. 2:4–10 | Eph. 2:4–10 | Eph. 2:4–10 | Eph. 2:1–10 | Eph. 2:1–10 |
| John 3:14–21 | John 3:14–21 | John 6:4–15 | John 3:14–21 | John 3:14–21 |

### FIRST LESSON: NUMBERS 21:4–9

The stories of the wandering in the wilderness include several episodes in which the people murmur and "test" God by demanding a change in the conditions of their life. New Testament writers used the murmuring of the wilderness generation as a warning to Christians. Paul warns the Corinthians that the destruction by serpents is a lesson for Christians that they should not test the Lord by indulging in idolatry (1 Cor. 10:6–12). This story was used in the Johannine tradition as a type for the life-giving salvation that comes through the cross.

The people complain against Moses for having led them out of Egypt to die in the wilderness. The bondage in Egypt and the celebration of the Exodus as liberation are all forgotten. They complain about the food which they have in the desert. Exegetes are not sure whether the author intends this complaint to be simply a reference to the meager type of food that one can find in the wilderness or whether it is intended to refer back to the manna, the food which God had provided (cf. 11:6). Since the manna had already been the object of complaint in 11:6, where the people then demanded meat and remembered all the vegetables that they had eaten in Egypt, it is possible that a reference to the earlier incident is intended. In that story God responds to Moses' prayer by providing quails. However, as the people are eating the quails, the Lord strikes them with a plague. In this story, the anger of the Lord is the immediate response to the people's complaint.

The story mentions two types of serpents: the poisonous, fiery serpent and the bronze serpent made by Moses. There is no explanation of what is meant by the fiery serpents (nehasim seraphim). Isa. 30:6 and 14:29 speak of flying serpents in the wilderness. The winged serpent also appears in the call vision of Isaiah (6:2, 6). According to 2 Kings 18:4, there was a bronze serpent made by Moses in the Temple, perhaps the serpent of Isaiah's vision. The Israelites are said to have offered sacrifice to the serpent until it was removed from the Temple as idolatrous by Hezekiah. The story itself presents the bronze serpent as a piece of "sympathetic magic": looking upon the bronze image of the serpent cures the effects of the poisonous snake bite. This healing may also reflect the widespread symbolism of the healing deity as a serpent. However, the author of Numbers does not leave the story at this level of magical healing. It is a tale of the people's disobedience and punishment; of their repentance and God's salvation. Their confession of sin and Moses' intercession mediate the event of divine salvation. The serpent is made in response to God's command. Those who are bitten must look upon it to attain life. Thus, the incident is transformed into a sign of the life-giving power of God, which is able to triumph over the hardships and dangers of the wilderness.

## SECOND LESSON: EPHESIANS 2:4-10

This passage contrasts the mercy of God with the sinfulness of humanity, which makes both Gentile and Jew deserving of divine wrath (vv. 1-3). We have already seen that this contrast is well-established in the Pauline tradition. This passage reflects the basic Pauline image of salvation through God's grace to an undeserving humanity, though it lacks the more characteristic language of righteousness through faith found in Romans. Instead, the author speaks of the graciousness of God. Another shift in language occurs when Ephesians speaks of the believer as raised with Christ. This image of the faithful raised with the exalted Christ to the heavens goes beyond the collapse of the categories of past, present, and future in the experience of salvation that we have already observed in Rom. 5:1–11. There, participation in divine glory remains firmly in the future. First Cor. 15:51–57 reserves the language of the resurrection of the faithful for the second coming.

However, 1 Cor. 15:57 can also speak of God giving the Christian the victory through Jesus Christ. We have also seen in Rom. 8:37 that Paul can describe the Christian life as one in which the Christian is able to conquer all hardships through God's salvation in Christ. Since Eph. 2:1–3 speaks in mythological terms of the passions which led to sin and death as showing Christians to have been under the power of "the prince of the air," the image of heavenly exaltation and victory over the powers of evil as participation in the exaltation of the risen Christ would form a natural way of expressing the significance of salvation.

As in Rom. 8:31–39, the salvation which comes to a humanity trapped in sin stems from the love of God for us. Eph. 2:4 opens its celebration of the victory of salvation by referring to the richness of divine mercy and the abundance of God's love. These attributes are not new insights into God's character. We have seen that mercy, faithfulness, and loving kindness are the fundamental characteristics of the God of the covenant traditions. Verses 3 and 4 back mercy and love up against the deserved response of divine wrath in a striking way. Verse 5 continues the contrast by immediately speaking of the former state of the believers as "being dead through our trespasses." The Jewish tradition had understood Genesis to mean that the sinfulness shown in Adam and in the story of the people's disobedience to God meant that humanity no longer shared the immortality for which it had been destined. The author is not concerned with life and death as they occur in the natural world. Death represents the separation from God caused by human sinfulness. Life implies life with God, a life which restores what had been lost in Adam. Ephesians attributes all these acts of salvation to God.

God saves those dead through sin in Christ. God raises and exalts them with Christ in the heavens (vv. 5b–6). The Christians are God's creation, created in Christ (v. 10). This imagery presents the Christian as God's new creation. Just as Paul does elsewhere, the author of Ephesians warns his readers against thinking that they have somehow merited such salvation. Verses 8–9 break into the lyrical celebration of salvation to drive this point home. Nothing that human beings could do merits redemption. Redemption is the free gift of God. The believer is saved by grace through faith and not through any works. Thus one cannot use one's "exaltation with Christ" as an occasion for boasting. In Romans Paul speaks against the boasting engendered by those who think that salvation depends upon "works of the law" (cf. 3:27–29). Ephesians does not specify what works are rejected. But the passage is primarily directed toward Gentile converts for whom "works of the law" were not a problem. Therefore, the author has generalized the expression as a warning against any tendency to boasting in one's ability to achieve salvation in some way.

Though some exegetes find in this passage a doctrine of baptismal resurrection or a gnostic vision of the soul's triumph over the powers of evil, it can be understood as an exposition of the Pauline tradition. Others have proposed that the ritual of baptism might have included an enthronement of the newly baptized that symbolized their new life and status. Such a rite would provide the foundation for the language of the passage. Ephesians is clearly exploiting the contrast between the present and past state of the believer in this passage.

However, the author is not merely describing salvation in terms of a cosmic victory. Ephesians sees that the new life that the Christian has also has a role in the larger divine plan. The Christian community of Gentile and Jew reflects God's new creation. As such, its task is to show forth the graciousness of God. Verse 7 points to the life of the Christian community with the risen Lord as showing ages to come the wealth of God's graciousness in Christ. In verse 10 we learn that this demonstration is expressed in "good works." These "good works" form the antithesis to the sins in which the believers walked before their conversion. However, the individual is not to take credit for any such accomplishments. Instead, Ephesians sees them as part of the larger divine plan, which had been laid down in the beginning. He speaks of them as works which God "prepared beforehand." The language of divine preparation presupposes an order to events that is working out a divine plan of salvation. Paul speaks of the vessels of divine mercy prepared beforehand in Rom. 9:23. However, the image of "good works" prepared beforehand is unusual. It serves the purpose of presenting the new creation as one in which persons walk as God intended, which implies doing good works without permitting individuals to think that they can take credit for such works. At the same time, this metaphor implies that the Christian community, which has come into being through Christ, has an important responsibility, since it must testify by its way of life to the graciousness of God. Salvation won in Christ must have an ethical translation in the life of the community. The experience of resurrection and exaltation with Christ is not hidden as some merely private or emotional experience. It issues in the good works that demonstrate God's graciousness and the freedom and new life won for the believer.

## GOSPEL: JOHN 3:14–21

This passage consists of two elements. Verses 14–15 are attached to Jesus' dialogue with Nicodemus (vv. 1–13) as a passion prediction that points toward the real salvation that is present in Jesus. Verses 16–21 are a discourse about the necessity of belief in Jesus for salvation. It summarizes basic themes and images of the Gospel. To an even more marked degree than Ephesians, the Johannine tradition sees salvation as present in the life of the believer. Much of the apocalyptic imagery of judgment is reapplied to the decisive point at which a person either comes to believe in Jesus or fails to do so.

Verses 14–15 are the first of three passion predictions in the Fourth Gospel. Like the synoptic tradition (Mark 8:31), the crucified is presented as Son of man, and the divine necessity of the passion is indicated by use of the expression *dei,* "it is necessary." The context of the passage points to Johannine transformations of the Son of man imagery. In v. 12 the evangelist hints that he is about to reveal "heavenly things" rather than the earthly ones that have been the topic of discourse with Nicodemus. For John such "heavenly things" all concern Jesus' identity with the Father or the necessity of salvation through belief in Jesus. Verse 13 rejects all other revealers by insisting that the only one who knows heavenly things is the one who has come down from heaven. No human can claim to have gone up into heaven. The Son of man is the one who has come down from heaven—that is, Jesus. The Jewish image of the Son of man in Dan. 7:14ff moves in the opposite direction. The "one like a son of man" ascends to the throne of God. Christian tradition spoke of the coming of Jesus as Son of man at the Parousia. Here John takes the coming of the Son of man to be the earthly ministry of Jesus, not the Parousia. For the Johannine tradition, Jesus' ascent to heaven is a return to the Father. It takes place in the crucifixion, which is consistently portrayed as Jesus' exaltation.

The divine necessity inherent in the crucifixion was often expressed by appealing to proof texts from the Old Testament. This passage turns to Num. 21:8–10, which is presented as a typology of the crucifixion. Instead of the healing, that is, return to natural life that one finds in the Old Testament story, belief in the crucified Son of man will bring eternal life, one of the Gospel's common images for salvation. Such typologies may have been a common feature of preaching in the Johannine church. John 6:30–58 provides an elaborate typology in which Jesus' word and then the Eucharist provide eternal life to the believer over against the manna given by Moses. As in this passage, Jesus' ability to provide such life is linked with the assertion that he is the one who has come down from heaven and gives his life to the world (6:33). The other two passion predictions in John also point to Jesus' divine identity and mission. John 8:28 directs a passion prediction against Jesus' Jewish opponents, "When you have lifted up the Son of man, you will know that I Am and that I do nothing on my own authority but I speak as the Father has commanded me." It combines Jesus' identity with the Father and the defense of his teaching as from God. Its setting in a controversy implies that those responsible for his crucifixion will be shown to have rejected God. John 12:32 promises that when Jesus is lifted up, he will draw the whole world to himself. Thus, the messianic prophecy of the coming of the Gentiles is to be fulfilled in the crucifixion. The "whoever believes" of John 3:15 has a universalist side in this prophecy.

The discourse in vv. 16–21 elaborates on the implications of v. 15. It begins with the assertion of God's love for the world as the basis of salvation (cf. John 6:33). This expression is unusual, since one usually finds the love of God directed toward the people of God, or toward the believers—that is, toward those who have experienced God's salvation. The latter way of speaking is not only typical of the Johannine tradition (e.g., 1 John 4:9) but also of the Pauline tradition as we have seen in Rom. 8:39 and Eph. 2:4. It is unusual because "the world" often appears as a negative symbol of all those who reject the revelation that comes with Jesus in the Fourth Gospel so that the world can be described as hating Jesus and his followers (15:18f). Verse 16 expresses in Johannine language a thought similar to that in Rom. 5:8. God's love for a sinful world is reflected in Jesus' death on the cross. "Giving" the Son reflects the language of crucifixion (Rom. 8:32; Gal. 2:20).

However, the Fourth Gospel does not focus its soteriology on the cross as the Pauline traditions do. Instead, the saving activity of the Son is associated with Jesus' revelation of the Father. That revelation begins with Jesus' coming into the world. Verse 17 makes that transition into Johannine categories of realized eschatology. We have seen that John reformulated the tradition of the Son of man coming in judgment to apply to Jesus' coming into the world. This reformulation is also evident in v. 17. The Son does not come into the world in order to judge or condemn but to save. However, John insists judgment does result from the Son's coming. Since it is necessary to believe in Jesus as the one sent from the Father in order to be saved, the person who does not believe is already condemned. For the Johannine tradition, belief is more than a positive response to Jesus' message; it contains an affirmation about Jesus himself that is a major point of controversy throughout the Gospel. Jesus is the only Son of the Father. The word for *only, monogenes,* expresses Jesus' uniqueness and his preciousness to God. It reflects the Hebrew word *yahid* that is used for Isaac in Gen. 22:2, 12, 16. Heb. 11:17 uses *monogenes* of Isaac. The implications of this relationship are spelled out in the Gospel. Jesus is the only one who reveals the Father, who knows heavenly things, who speaks with God's authority. He can even be identified with God.

Verses 19–21 explain what the Johannine tradition means by judgment in language that is reminiscent of the dualism of Jewish apocalyptic. Light stands opposed to darkness. Humanity is divided into two camps, those whose evil deeds show them to belong to darkness and those whose good deeds show that they belong to the light. John uses this anthropological dualism to explain the twofold reaction to Jesus. Those who practice evil love darkness and hate the light. They will not respond to anything that comes from God. The righteous person, on the other hand, will seek the light. In dividing humanity in this way, John provides an explanation for why some respond with such violence against Jesus. Jesus, as light, shows what persons really are. The Fourth Gospel has such a strong identification of Jesus and God that it does not envisage the possibility that rejection of Jesus could be anything but sinful. To reject Jesus is to reject God. Such people have condemned themselves.

All three readings juxtapose the divine judgment that is due a sinful humanity with the divine love that steps in to save that humanity. Though one might be tempted to read the story in Numbers simply as one of judgment, the Johannine tradition found it to be a typology of salvation. The people's disbelief and complaints merited God's punishment. Yet, upon their repentance and Moses' intercession, God provided healing. Ephesians emphasizes the fact that God's salvation in Christ comes to those who are dead in their trespasses. There is no possibility that humanity might earn salvation as the reward for its own obedience. Salvation can only come to those who believe.

The Johannine tradition takes up traditional themes in its own way. It agrees that Jesus' death is the fundamental sign of God's love for a sinful world. But the realized eschatology of the Johannine tradition leads the author to radicalize the language of judgment. A person's response to Jesus writes his or her judgment, either eternal life or condemnation. Thus, the extraordinary outpouring of divine love in Christ has its other side. The picture of judgment becomes even more somber, since it includes the possibility of some persons cutting themselves off from that salvation. The judgment is now, John tells his readers; not in some distant future.

Ephesians reminds the Christian community of its special responsibility in God's plan of salvation. That community must be a sign of the lovingkindness of God, which it has experienced. The language of judgment is not aimed at discouraging the believer; indeed, Ephesians speaks of the victory over evil powers in the most exalted symbolism—sharing the life and exaltation of the risen Christ. Rather, it should serve to remind the Christian that the faith which he or she has is not a personal accomplishment to be taken for granted or something in which one may boast. Instead, it is a gift of God for which one is to be thankful. Part of that response is implied in the language of walking in good works, since these works are to show the graciousness of God.

# The Fifth Sunday in Lent

| Lutheran | Roman Catholic | Episcopal | Pres/UCC/Chr | Meth/COCU |
|----------|----------------|-----------|--------------|-----------|
| Jer. 31:31–34 | Jer. 31:31–34 | Jer. 31:31–34 | Jer. 31:31–34 | Jer. 31:31–34 |
| Heb. 5:7–9 | Heb. 5:7–9 | Heb. 5:1–4 | Heb. 5:7–10 | Heb. 5:7–10 |
| John 12:20–33 | John 12:20–33 | John 12:20–33 | John 12:20–33 | John 12:20–33 |

### FIRST LESSON: JEREMIAH 31:31–34

This passage owes its significance to the Christian claim that the new covenant of which it speaks has been brought about through Jesus (Luke 22:20; Heb. 8:8–12; 2 Cor. 3:6–8). Jeremiah reflects upon the history of Israel's disobedience and the hostile reception accorded his own message and that of the great prophets before him. This reflection leads him to raise the question of human obedience to God in a radical way. Is it perhaps impossible for the human to be faithful to the covenant? Jeremiah also saw his earlier prophecies of doom fulfilled in the Babylonian exile. This experience might have led to cynical discouragement. Instead, he turns to prophecies of salvation for those who survive the terrible trials of the exile. Not only will those who have recently been taken away from Judah be restored but also those who were taken from the North in the Assyrian invasions of two centuries earlier (v. 27).

The promise of a new covenant with Israel and Judah envisages a radical end to the story of disobedience which had typified the relationship between Yahweh and the people. Jer. 11:1–11 contrasts the obedience called for by the Exodus covenant as the condition of its blessings with the stubborn heart in which the people have chosen to walk. Consequently, they have deserved to suffer the curses of the covenant. The people seem no more capable of doing good than a leopard of changing its spots (13:23). Though the old covenant was supported by the great act of liberation of the people from Egypt and by God's acting as husband toward Israel, it was still broken. The covenant between God and the people after the exile cannot be like the old covenant.

Verses 33–34 turn to the new covenant. Yahweh must undertake a new act in which the law is put within the hearts of the people (v. 33a). Jer. 17:1 spoke of the sin of the people being engraved upon its heart. This promise reverses that picture of sinfulness. Verse 33b recalls the formula of association between the Lord and the people, "I will be their God and they will be my people." This expression may reflect the opening of the Decalogue (Exod. 20:2). Its frequency in Jeremiah suggests that it was a well-known phrase (7:23; 11:4; 24:7; 31:1; 32:38; also see Ezek. 11:20; 36:28). The image of the law being within the hearts of the people also occurs in Deut. 6:6 and 30:14. There the presence of the law in the heart makes it possible for a person to perform what is set out in the law. However, Deut. 6:7 presumes that a person with the law in his or her heart must teach that law to his or her children. Jer. 31:34a envisages a situation in which the necessity of teaching the law is transcended. Everyone in the nation will know that Lord. Deut. 30:5–6 comes closest to this sentiment when it speaks of the Lord circumcising the hearts of Israel and her descendants. Thus this passage in Jeremiah expresses a sentiment about the renewal of the people that was strongly felt in various quarters of the exilic community. The depths of human disobedience and sinfulness had been revealed in the tragic events of the exile. Remembering the story of the people from the Exodus generation to its present, the community could see that its story had been one of disobedience and blindness.

Verse 34b knows that it is still possible to look to a God who can erase all the iniquity of the people, to one who will no longer remember her sin. God may yet bring Israel to faithfulness and obedi-

ence. Thus the new covenant is a great promise of hope and salvation
to a community that is able to see the disaster of its own story of
sinfulness and disobedience.

Most of us are probably fairly sympathetic with Jeremiah's rather
pessimistic view of human nature. But we usually use that view to
excuse ourselves and others. For Jeremiah, on the other hand, however natural disobedience may be in the human story, it still merits the
divine punishment it receives. At the same time, Jeremiah does not
become cynical, since it is always possible for God to make a new
covenant. This possibility is rooted in the conviction that God intends
to be the God of this people. God will not give up on the covenant
people no matter what they may do. Even in the disasters of the exile
the seeds of salvation are already being sown.

### SECOND LESSON: HEBREWS 5:7–10

These verses conclude a description of Jesus as High Priest according to the order of Melchizedek that began at 4:14. The argument in
Hebrews is addressed to Christians who sought to retain some form of
Jewish cultic practice. Scholars have argued that Hebrews is directed
toward Jewish Christians, who wished to see Christianity as a sect of
Judaism. While Jewish traditions of the first century viewed Melchizedek as a heavenly deliverer of Israel and as a sign of the perma-
nent validity of the Levitical priesthood, Hebrews uses the figure of
Melchizedek to argue for an order of priesthood superior to the
priesthood of the Jewish cult. This priesthood is realized in the
once-for-all sacrifice that Jesus has offered for sin. Having entered
into heaven through this sacrifice, Jesus remains there as a sympathetic intercessor for those who appeal to him (4:14–16). All of the cultic
practices of the OT are merely shadows of this offering. Consequently, Hebrews argues, they have now lost their validity.

Hebrews combines images from Jewish apocalyptic with the language of Platonic mysticism as it was used by some Jews to interpret
the OT. The latter sees the realities in heaven to be the true realities, of
which things in the world are mere copies. It finds in the stories of
Moses and the patriarchs examples of the education of the soul in
virtue, so that it can overcome the passions which bind it to this earth
and enjoy the vision of the heavenly realities and friendship with God

through divine wisdom. God's wisdom, or Word, was said to dwell in the soul of such persons. Hebrews applies these categories to Christ in a striking way. The tradition spoke of the wisdom, or Word, as God's image, through which God creates and sustains the world and through which God's presence comes to the souls of the pious. Hebrews opens with a vision of Christ as the image of God, who makes sacrifice for sins and then returns to God, where he is exalted above all the powers of the universe (1:1–4).

Hebrews makes important revisions in its use of Platonic categories. The heavenly realities were thought to be eternal and unchanging. The soul of the virtuous person became like them in freeing itself from passions. In the first verse of Hebrews we find the eternal image of God making satisfaction for sin and returning to heaven. Such an involvement with the changing realities of the material world would be unthinkable to a Platonist. Hebrews will claim that it is the source of Christ's superiority to the angels and the other powers of the world. Our passage presses this point home in connection with the understanding of Jesus as High Priest. Heb. 4:15 describes this heavenly High Priest as able to sympathize with those who seek his aid. This expression forms a sharp contrast to the passion-free state of the soul. The verse attributes this sympathy to the fact that Christ has been tested in all things as we are but is without sin. We often presume quite the opposite. We think that Christ is like the wise person of the Platonic tradition. His soul is completely under the control of the divine Word, so that it really makes no sense to think of Christ as experiencing the kind of testing and temptation to which we are subject. Hebrews is asserting the opposite. In this connection the only difference between the experience of other humans and that of Christ is that Christ did not sin. In 4:16, Hebrews argues that this likeness in temptation or testing provides the basis for our confidence in the mercy, grace, and assistance that we will receive from God.

Verses 7–9 return to the theme of Christ's testing. Verse 10 rounds out the section by concluding that it is this Christ whom God has established as High Priest. Although it is not possible to link vv. 7–8 to one of the accounts of Jesus' agony in Gethsemane, there is clearly a link between these verses and a tradition of Jesus' agony in the face of his impending passion. The Johannine churches also know an independent tradition of the agony of Jesus that was not linked with a scene in the Garden of Gethsemane. Hebrews speaks of this appeal to God occurring "in the days of his flesh," that is, during his lifetime. The author wishes us to see this example as the culmination of the testing and education in the weaknesses of humanity that Jesus has undergone.

The description of God as the one who is able to rescue the righteous person from death is common in the OT (see Hos. 13:14; Ps. 33:19). However, Hebrews is not dependent solely upon the OT picture of the righteous person and the traditions of Jesus' agony. Hellenistic Jewish traditions presented the wise person as one who is able to cry out to God with a loud voice. Thus, the emphasis upon the loud cries and tears is not a sign of weakness on Jesus' part. It is a sign of his closeness to God. The author makes it clear that he is speaking out of that tradition when he concludes that "he was heard on account of his piety." The agony traditions do not show Jesus as weak in our sense that temptation or testing is something that afflicts the weak person. They show him as the truly pious person.

The soul of the wise person was described as undergoing an education in virtue. Verse 8 applies that view to Jesus. He learned obedience through his sufferings. Phil. 2:8 speaks of Christ humbling himself and becoming obedient to the point of death. Hebrews may reflect a similar passion tradition in this verse. It contrasts Jesus' exalted status as "Son" with the obedience learned in suffering.

Verse 9 brings this language of an education in suffering and Jesus as the model of the pious, wise person to its conclusion. Through this process, Jesus has "been perfected." The language of perfection in Hebrews embraces the three traditions of piety: the cultic, which sees perfection in the holiness of the sanctuary; the apocalyptic, which speaks of what is perfect coming with the Messiah; and the Platonic, which speaks of the soul of the wise person as perfect. The combination of meanings is already apparent in Heb. 2:9–10. Jesus, now exalted in heaven, tasted death for everyone. He is identified with the eternal divine image active in creation and at the same time is the leader of many to divine glory because he was perfected in suffering. The entry of the righteous into glory with the Messiah is an apocalyptic concept. The language of divine image comes from the Platonic tradition. The connection with the language of priesthood in our passage introduces the cultic sense of perfection. This cultic meaning will be elaborated in Platonic terms in Heb. 7:26–28. There the perfection and eternity of what is in the heavens is applied to the sinlessness and once-for-all character of the Son and his offering.

Hebrews draws a striking picture of Christ as the source of our salvation. The Platonic image of the wise person is perhaps strange to us. Yet we retain elements of it in our images of Jesus. We may think of him as unable to sympathize with human weaknesses because he cannot really experience what we do. Or we may have an image of perfection that is closer to the passionless state of soul than to the education through sufferings which Hebrews envisages. Such visions of perfection create a barrier between ourselves and God even if we are not conscious of it. They make God's perfection so antithetical to the reality of human life as we experience it that we can only hope that God will hear our prayer. Hebrews insists that one can describe Jesus as the divine image becoming educated in the realities of human experience. Jesus' sinlessness and exaltation with God do not separate him from us but serve to guarantee that the salvation won in Jesus is "once for all." It will not have to be repeated or complemented by some other ritual. Thus, Hebrews consistently exhorts us to pray with confidence in the sympathy that we will receive from God.

### GOSPEL: JOHN 12:20–33

This passage begins with a truncated scene in which some Greeks (= Gentiles) come asking to see Jesus (vv. 20–22). That incident serves as the catalyst for a discourse in which Jesus announces the arrival of the "hour," that is, the time of his passion. Throughout the Gospel we have been told that Jesus' hour is not yet (2:4; 7:6, 8, 30; 8:20). Now Jesus' public teaching is concluded with the proclamation that the hour of his glorification has come. The final prediction of the passion as the lifting up of the Son of man (12:32) predicts that the crucified will "draw all to himself." In other early Christian traditions, we find the theme of the Jewish rejection of Jesus making the great conversion of the Gentiles possible (cf. Rom. 11:7–12). John has used a story in which Greeks came to Jesus as his introduction to the announcement of the hour. The original story presumably concluded with an exchange between Jesus and the Greeks as in the synoptic tradition of Jesus' encounter with the Syrophoenician woman (Mark 7:24–30). Here such an exchange is unnecessary. The assurance that the Greeks can be saved is given in the passion prediction. Indeed, their coming to see Jesus is a sign that the hour has arrived.

Verse 23 announces that it is the hour for the Son of man to be glorified. The reader of the Gospel knows that the glorification of Jesus takes place upon the cross. It is the point of the Son's exaltation and return to the Father.

Verses 24–26 interrupt the glorification theme with a collection of sayings about suffering and discipleship. Verse 24 uses a proverbial association between the death of a seed in the ground and its productivity. The connection between the sowing of seeds and productivity is the subject of seed parables in the synoptic tradition (for example, Mark 4:3–8). John may have reapplied such a parable to the death of Jesus. The coming of the Greeks is symbolic of the "much fruit" to come. He has included a related saying in the context of the Samaritan mission when he points to the abundance of the harvest (4:35f).

Verses 25 and 26 contain Johannine variants of sayings with parallels in Mark 8:34f. The saying about losing and saving one's life circulated widely in early Christianity (Luke 9:24; 17:33; Matt. 10:39; 16:25). The Johannine version of the saying in verse 25 speaks of loving or hating life rather than of saving or seeking to preserve it as we find in the synoptics. The antithesis of love/hate may go back to the missionary context of such sayings. In Matthew's editing of these sayings for missionaries (Matt. 10:37–39), we find the saying about loving family more than Jesus making one unworthy to be a disciple used to introduce the sayings on following Jesus. This short collection of sayings about suffering and discipleship may have been used as missionary instruction in the Johannine community as well.

The final saying in John's collection (v. 26) speaks of the person who wishes to "serve" Jesus rather than to "come after" as in the synoptic sayings. The injunction to take up one's cross is not found here. These shifts may represent the generalizing of the saying to apply to all disciples. The conclusion to the saying (v. 26bc) presents the promise of salvation in characteristically Johannine terms. Jesus' servant will be with him and will be honored by the Father. These themes are repeated in various ways in the discourses at the Last Supper (14:3, 21, 23; 17:24).

The theme of glorification returns in vv. 27–30. These verses also contain traditions that reflect an agony of Jesus. The Johannine tradition has a citation of Ps. 6.4f rather than Ps. 42:6 as in Matt. 26:38. John has reformulated the agony tradition so that it becomes an explicit denial of the possibility that Jesus might seek to be spared the hour for which he has come into the world (for example, 3:16). The prayer in v. 28 is characteristic of Jesus throughout the events of the passion. Jesus asks that the Father's name be glorified. This passage is a Johannine version of the petition in the Lord's Prayer that God's name be sanctified and his will be done (Matt. 6:10). Matthew uses the expression "thy will be done" in his Gethsemane scene (26:42). For John, Jesus' entire ministry has been the glorification of the Father. This glorification reaches its climax when Jesus announces as he dies on the cross that the work the Father gave him to do has been completed (19:30). Jesus will pray for the glorification of the Father's name twice more. In 13:31f he proclaims that the Son of man has been glorified and the Father has been glorified in him. In 17:1–5 Jesus prays to the Father to glorify him with the glory that he had before the beginning of the world. This glory is linked with the salvation that comes to all who believe in the Son. John 17:4 affirms that Jesus has glorified the Father in accomplishing what the Father sent him to do. John 17:24 asks that the disciples will be with Jesus and will behold his glory.

The second half of v. 28 has the divine voice from heaven affirm that God has glorified and will glorify the name as Jesus requests. Since the Fourth Gospel does not have a Transfiguration scene, exegetes have suggested that this manifestation of the divine voice is the Johannine version of the transfiguration. Johannine narrative typically has affirmations of Jesus' relationship with the Father followed by statements in which the opinions of the crowd are given (v. 29). These opinions are usually divided between those who reject what happened and those whose views represent a partial faith that is inadequate from the evangelist's point of view. The first group attribute the rumble to thunder. The second group thinks that an angel has spoken. Their opinion is closer to the truth because it attributes the voice to a heavenly being. However, it is finally wrong because it does not perceive that the Father speaks directly to Jesus.

The intent of v. 30 is problematic. John 11:41f has Jesus pray to the Father to set an example for the crowd, but it is difficult to see what the examplary character of this episode would be. If one takes v. 30 with v. 31, then it becomes a sign that the hour of divine judgment is at hand. John reinterprets the Parousia expectations of early Christianity to refer to the encounter with Jesus. Verse 31 contains such an interpretation: the decisive victory over Satan is won when the Son is glorified on the cross. This affirmation has its parallels in the exaltation traditions elsewhere in the New Testament. Phil. 2:6–11 and Heb. 1:3–4 envisage the risen Christ enthroned over the powers of the cosmos. Eph. 2:4–10 described the Christian as enthroned with the victorious Christ as well. John 14:30f refers to the coming passion as Jesus' encounter with the ruler of this world. Satan has no power over Jesus because Jesus is perfectly obedient to the Father. These traditions do not naively assume that sin has been eradicated from the world or from the lives of Christians. But they insist that the hold that it has over humanity has been decisively broken.

This announcement of the defeat of Satan serves to introduce the final prediction of the lifting up of the Son of man in John 12:32. From the two earlier passion predictions the reader knows that belief in the crucified is the source of eternal life, that Jesus exalted on the cross reveals the divine "I Am," and that the cross proves that Jesus has always been perfectly obedient to the Father. Jesus' exaltation on the cross makes him the Savior of the world.

As in other passages of John, we find a variety of reactions to Jesus. We are not told what drew the Greeks in the opening scene. However, the passion prediction indicates that only the person who sees God's glory in the crucified Jesus can really be said to have come to Jesus. The sayings on discipleship point to the close association between those who follow Jesus and the Father. Their eternal life is with Jesus and the Father. Finally, the crowd represents the spectrum of reactions which are inadequate. One group perceives the divine voice as mere thunder. Another perceives Jesus as the sort of holy person to whom an angel might speak. But they do not have any hint of his special relationship to the Father. John, which goes even further than

Hebrews in portraying Jesus' identity as divine Son of God, still insists upon the reality of Jesus' obedience. As in Hebrews, that reality is preserved in the tradition of Jesus' agony before the passion. Jesus is not the unwilling victim of human plots against him. He is not coerced to his doom by a divine power that he cannot resist, as the victim of a Greek tragedy might be. He is not even the victim of Satan's power over the world. The passion represents the deliberate choice of a destiny by which Jesus glorifies God.

One literary critic has commented that the Bible is built on an unrelieved tension between the most direct realism in portraying the flaws in human nature and the most persistent optimism in proclaiming that sin, imperfection, and meaninglessness are not the final reading of human destiny. These readings that look forward to the events of Holy Week and Easter are no exception. Jeremiah's vision of a new covenant born out of the devastating experiences of the exile shows an extraordinary confidence in God's ability to once again renew a sinful people.

The NT images of Jesus' confrontation with his hour in Hebrews and John show the vicious cycle of sin broken in the obedience of the cross. Hebrews speaks in cultic language of a sin offering that will never have to be repeated and of a compassionate, eternal High Priest in Jesus. John uses an apocalyptic metaphor of the decisive defeat of Satan by God's Messiah. Rather than a universal change of the human heart such as one might imagine on the basis of Jeremiah, God takes on human weakness and suffering in the Son. His obedience makes salvation possible for those who believe. The Gospel presents us with the believer as the one who serves Jesus, who shares his relationship to the world, and who will also be with the Father as he is. We often allow the "realistic" images of human weakness and sinfulness to talk us out of the images of salvation. The optimism shown by the biblical tradition is not grounded in an assessment of our human capacities but in the conviction that God has acted to save us as human beings. We are challenged by the biblical tradition to respond accordingly, not to languish in a complacent acceptance of weakness, sinfulness, and imperfection.